Ask the Right Question

TIPS AND TECHNIQUES

TO TRANSFORM YOUR KEY SKILLS

AND RELATIONSHIPS

Rupert Eales-White

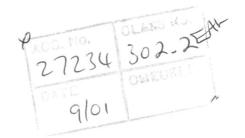
The McGraw-Hill Companies

London · New York · St Louis · San Francisco · Auckland
Bogotá · Caracas · Lisbon · Madrid · Mexico · Milan
Montreal · New Delhi · Panama · Paris · San Juan
São Paulo · Singapore · Sydney · Tokyo · Toronto

Published by
McGRAW-HILL Publishing Company
Shoppenhangers Road, Maidenhead, Berkshire SL6 2QL, England
Telephone 01628 502500
Fax 01628 770224

British Library Cataloguing in Publication Data
Eales-White, Rupert
   Ask the right question: tips and techniques to transform your
   key skills and relationships
   1. Questioning   2. Oral communication   3. Communication in
   management
   I. Title
   302.2'242

   ISBN 0-07-709268-6

Library of Congress Cataloging-in-Publication Data
Eales-White, Rupert.
   Ask the right question: tips and techniques to transform your key
   skills and relationships / Rupert Eales-White.
      p.   cm.
   Includes index.
   ISBN 0-07-709268-6 (pbk. : alk. paper)
   1. Business communication.   2. Questioning.   3. Conversation.
   I. Title.
   HF5718.E18   1997
   650.1'3–dc20
                                                                                96-46516
                                                                                CIP

McGraw-Hill

A Division of The McGraw·Hill Companies

12345 CUP 9987

Typeset by BookEns Ltd., Royston, Herts.
and printed and bound in Great Britain at the University Press, Cambridge

Printed on permanent paper in compliance with ISO Standard 9706

Ask the Right Question

Contents

Introduction

Have you ever left a meeting or concluded a conversation feeling that you hadn't handled things properly or didn't get the answers you needed or expected? If you have, then this book is for you. The core reason for negative or unsatisfactory outcomes in conversations and relationships is failure to 'ask the right question'. We all fail in this regard, because we have never been taught the art and science of effective questioning.

Part I of this book, therefore, focuses on 'What are the right questions?' and 'How we can ask them at the right time in the right way to produce the right result?'. The focus is on conversation that not only improves the relationship, but also the outputs of the relationship—the actions that both parties can take to solve problems or create and seize opportunities in our business and personal worlds. Good questioning and effective listening, covered in the second chapter, will transform our relationships and improve key skills, enabling us to become more assertive, more creative, more persuasive and more effective interviewers. Each of these areas is covered in Part II of the book: 'How to develop key skills.'

However, this book covers more than just questioning, listening and applying them successfully to improve key skills and relationships. I have been privileged over the past six years to facilitate learning in the areas of interviewing, persuading, creative thinking, assertiveness and dealing with 'bosses', 'followers' and clients. I have also had conversations with many managers and executives from a wide range of companies, industries and countries. With few exceptions, the issue of greatest personal concern is the relationship with the boss, who is a key figure in our careers, followed by the relationship with clients, who produce the business for us and, finally, the relationship with 'subordinates', who help us meet our targets.

Another key issue that is common to many such conversations is 'meetings'. The general experience is that meetings are far too numerous, often wasting everyone's time and forcing the individual manager to work longer hours to catch up or stay ahead than would otherwise be necessary.

These conversations have produced a number of tips and techniques, which form the heart of Chapter 7, 'How to run an effective meeting' (based on a case study of a manager, running effective meetings in her business world), and Part III, which examines the three pivotal relationships at work: boss, subordinate and client. Part III focuses not on the use of questions to improve relationships, as that will already have been covered in earlier parts, but on answers to key questions. In Chapter 9, we consider why the relationship with the boss is so important; we consider what our objectives should be, what can stop us having an effective relationship and what we need to do to ensure that we have the relationship that meets our objectives.

When looking at the relationship with subordinates in Chapter 10, we consider how we shall benefit if we have an effective relationship, what is required from us, as leaders, to produce that relationship, and how, without realizing it, we can generate significant gaps in perception between how we intend to behave, the way we manifest that intention and the impact it actually has on our followers. We consider how to close those gaps and how to ensure that we carry out quality appraisals with our subordinates, as that is a key occasion when we can develop an effective relationship.

In the final chapter, 'How to delight your client', we consider all the steps we need to take from first contact to long-term partnership, focusing on tips and techniques to ensure that we avoid the pitfalls that lie in wait.

Throughout the book, we use real conversations and real issues with real people to demonstrate the power of asking the right question and finding the right answers. The book will therefore help you frame the right questions and find the answers that meet your skill, relationship and career needs.

Rupert Eales-White

Part I
WHAT IS THE RIGHT
QUESTION?

What is the key to an effective conversation?

What this chapter covers

In this first chapter, we look at a number of real-life situations and conversations from two perspectives: conversations that go badly and ones that go well. We then look at a specific real-life problem and consider how it was solved, before turning to the initial analysis of what works and why.

Conversations that are ineffective or effective

We shall look at a series of conversations, beginning with the shorter conversation that is ineffective, followed by the longer conversation that is effective. We consider three specific situations, the first commencing with a managing director (MD) talking to a manager face-to-face followed by the manager relaying the MD's instructions to a subordinate face-to-face; the second is a telephone conversation between a mother and her teenage daughter; and the third is a face-to-face meeting between a boss and a subordinate.

MD/manager/subordinate

Ineffective

The MD called Tim into his office. So Tim duly went to his MD's office.

'Well Tim,' said the MD, 'I have come to a decision.'

'I see,' replied Tim, 'and what is that decision?'

'You are to transfer Charles from service delivery to selling with immediate effect.'

Tim was slightly stunned, then blurted out: 'But Charles doesn't like selling.'

The MD laughed in genuine amusement. 'Come on Tim. If the business world was run on the basis of the likes and dislikes of the people working in it, it would crumble around us. Sometimes I would like to do certain things and not do other things. I haven't got the luxury of doing what I like or not doing what I don't like. I have to do what is right, and so do you and so does Charles. Get on with it man—it's for the good of the company.'

With that the MD turned away from Tim and picked up the phone. The 'discussion' was at an end. Tim hovered a moment and left.

Tim was not an happy man. 'Charles will not take kindly to this at all,' he mused, 'but what can I do. The old man's word is law.' He decided to get it over with as quickly as possible. 'I too can show firm leadership.' So, having first telephoned Personnel with the news, he telephoned Charles and asked him to come round to his office straight-away. He felt a bit uncomfortable, and hoped he could manage the discussion quickly, efficiently and painlessly.

'Ah! Charles. Thanks for coming round. I have some excellent news for you. The MD is delighted with the ability you have shown in selling, and so you are to move into sales full-time, starting on Monday. Pauline at Personnel will sort out all the details for you. Congratulations, Charles, congratulations.' Tim shook Charles's hand vigorously and propelled him towards the door. 'If you have any teething problems, just come to see me. You know I'm always here to help.' A few seconds later, he was able to close the door behind the departing Charles. 'Well, well,' he thought, 'that wasn't too bad, at all—better than I expected. I'm a pretty good leader myself. I'll make MD ahead of that slime-ball Patrick.'

Charles walked slowly towards the toilets—he couldn't face his colleagues in the open plan office. He shook his head slightly in stunned surprise and temporary disbelief. He locked himself in the toilet and sat for a while on the seat, saying nothing but with a slight glistening in his eyes. Then, if you could have been there, you would have caught a few words, spoken softly but with passionate intensity. 'The bastards! The bloody bastards.'

Effective

The MD called John into his office. So John duly went to his MD's office.

'Well John,' said the MD, 'I have come to a decision.'

'I see', replied John, 'and what is that decision?'

'You are to transfer Charles from service delivery to selling with immediate effect.'

'May I ask what are the reasons behind this decision?'

'It's simple', replied the MD. 'I was talking to Joe Rainey from Bustables yesterday, and he mentioned how happy he was with Charles and how

Charles had managed to cross-sell some significant more business with them. Now that led me to thinking. As you know, John, I like to consider the implications of any information I get, just to see if I can produce something that will benefit our company.

'Well, it struck me that we have quality staff in service delivery, but our salesmen are a mixed bunch, with one or two poor performers. We need to strengthen sales, but, as you know, Group head office has a world-wide ban on any recruitment this year. So, as Charles is good at selling, it is important at this moment in time, with recovery on the way and our capacity high, that we strengthen sales. Answer, switch Charles, and there is enough capacity in delivery to handle Charles's loss.'

'That's a very sound move, David. May I suggest that we allow Charles a three-month transition period so that he is fully trained up for a more aggressive selling role, and he adjusts to the change better, and so performs better as a result', said John.

'Well I don't believe in mollycoddling our staff, as you know', came the instant reply from the MD. John said nothing. 'Well, OK, if you think so', the MD eventually continued. 'I'll leave the details to you. That's your job, after all. But make sure he is fully on board sooner rather than later, and certainly within three months.'

'Of course I will, David', agreed John, and left.

John felt a twinge of annoyance at this sudden turn of events. 'I am responsible for both sales and service delivery', he mused, 'but then the Old Man has come up with a sound idea. Perhaps I should have thought of it myself. I have been a bit too busy recently in day-to-day management— need to find time to stand back a bit and review things from a strategic perspective.

'It's going to be a bit tricky as I know that Charles is not too keen on selling, though he makes the occasional sale, following on from his own good work. Thank God I got a transition period, and thank God I have my quarterly review meeting with Charles on Friday. I won't need to surprise him at a special, unexpected meeting. Hey ho, I must away and plan my approach to Charles.'

So John spent a bit of time thinking through how he would approach the review meeting, given this new development. We pick up the conversation at the Friday meeting, as John broaches the subject with Charles.

'So, Charles, let's consider how your role should best develop in the next year or so. As a starting point, let us look at what you do well. What are your views?'

'Well, er,' Charles commenced after a short pause to gather his thoughts; 'delivering the service to the client. The exact nature of the service and timing of delivery is agreed in the proposal I get. I know our services backwards, my communication skills are good and I satisfy the client according to the agreed contract. What's more, I enjoy it, and the clients know I do, and that makes the service I provide even better.'

'Agreed', said John. 'There is no doubt that you perform very well in meeting the client's service needs. But what about selling? You do well there too.'

'Well I don't do much selling. And what I do is not proper selling', came Charles's reply.

'What do you mean precisely?' John asked.

'Well, the business I get is nearly all from existing clients, where I have already proved my competence, and who appreciate our company. So it is easy to sell more of the same service or sell different services that my colleagues actually deliver. I do not, like the full-time sales staff, follow up leads that come in via the telephone sales teams. That's not my role, and, what's more, I'm not an aggressive, pushy type.'

'No, you certainly are not', agreed John. 'Let me ask you. Why do our customers buy our services?'

Charles paused before replying: 'Because they believe that our service will meet their needs, and will provide value for money spent.'

'And who creates that belief?' was the next question from John.

'Well the salesperson, of course', came the instant reply from Charles.

'And how does the salesperson create that belief, without which there will be no purchase decision?' John continued probing.

'He builds the relationship and creates trust in himself as well as the service.' Charles was getting absorbed in the discussion.

'Yes, a good salesperson sells himself. Most service decisions or employment decisions for that matter are made as a direct result of the quality of the relationship the salesperson or the prospective employee creates with the purchaser. People buy people not products. You have excellent skills in communication and developing relationships. So, Charles, are you a good salesperson?'

'Well, put like that, the answer must be yes', came Charles's reply. 'I hadn't really thought about it before in those terms. But, yes, you are right. I am a good salesperson, but I prefer delivering the service.'

'Naturally so,' said John, 'as you are good at that, comfortable with it and spend most of your time working in that area. But there is something else to consider. In your opinion, how many competent service deliverers do we have?'

'Well,' mused Charles, 'I think the whole team is competent, one reason why we are getting so much repeat business.'

'I agree. What about good salespersons, taking the definition we have agreed?' asked John.

'Well, quite a few aren't up to scratch. Organizationally, we are better at delivery than selling', replied Charles.

'Again, I agree', said John. 'So, from an organizational perspective, which is the priority—finding a good salesperson or a good deliverer?'

'Well, obviously, a good salesperson.' Charles was following the logic quickly now, and was sitting back in his chair in a very relaxed position. Then he paused for a moment or two, leaned forward and with some animation said: 'Just a minute, I begin to see where all this is leading. You want me to do more selling, don't you?'

'Got it in one, Charles,' John smiled, 'and not just me, but our beloved MD as well.'

The conversation continues.

Charles felt he would like to take a brisk walk around the block before returning to the open plan office. He did so. When he returned he felt positive overall about the change. There was still an edge of discomfort, but that was more than balanced by a growing feeling of excitement and commitment.

Mother and 13-year-old daughter on telephone

Ineffective

Mother (M): So how was school?
Daughter (D): S'all right.
M: Do anything interesting?
D: Nup.
    [*Awkward pause.*]
M: I'll be home by 8 o'clock. See you then. Bye.
D: Bye.
M: [*Sadly, to herself.*] I just don't seem able to talk to Jenny these days.

Effective

Mother (M): So how was school, dear?
Daughter (D): S'all right.
M: So, what was the most exciting event of the day?
D: [*Pause.*] Well, Mum, spotty Johnny was sent to the headmaster by Miss Brown during our Maths lesson.
M: Oh! I see. So why was that?
D: Because she saw him hit Adam, and she sent him straight to the headmaster. You know how strict the school is on no hitting by anyone. In fact, we didn't see Johnny again that day. The rumour is that he has been suspended.
M: And do you think that is a fair decision, if the rumour turns out to be right?

D: Oh, no, Mum—completely wrong—but that's teachers for you.

M: So, Miss Brown must have missed something—jumped to the wrong conclusion. What did she miss?

D: It's like this Mum. Adam is an absolute pain—he's always teasing the girls and being generally horrible. In fact, he had just made my best friend Lucy cry by teasing her about her braces and poking her in the tummy. Johnny told him to stop it or else. Adam continued and he got what he deserved. But blind Miss Brown missed all that was going on, only saw Johnny hit Adam—and it was only a gentle slap—Adam played it up for all it was worth. Then Miss Brown, without asking for any explanation or finding out any facts, sends him off to the headmaster. We all feel very sorry for Johnny.

M: Well, that does seem unfair. What do you think can be done about it?

D: Dunno. [*Pause.*] Well, I suppose that if a few of us went to see Miss Brown tomorrow and explained what really happened, she might listen and do something. Could do that I suppose. I'll phone Mary, Lucy, and Bob tonight and see what they think. I wouldn't talk to Miss Brown on my own. I'll get onto that straight after Neighbours.

    What time are you coming home, Mum?

M: I'll be back by 8 at the latest—so I'll see you then.

D: OK Mum. I'll tell you what me mates say about seeing Miss Brown. Bye.

M: Bye.

Boss/subordinate

Ineffective

Boss (B): Chris tells me that you were late again this morning. Is that correct?

Subordinate (S): Yes. I'm very sorry.

B: In fact, you were half-an-hour late. Am I right?

S: Yes [*mumbled*].

B: To be completely accurate (and you know that I like to have my facts right), you have been half-an-hour late every day this week, have you not?

S: Yes.

B: Well, this firm does not tolerate laziness and unpunctuality. I am a fair man (as you know), but I don't beat about the bush. If this occurs once more, we will start the disciplinary procedures against you. Do I make myself clear?

S: Yes.

B: Well, don't let it happen again.

Effective

Boss (B): Chris tells me that you were half-an-hour late this morning, and, in fact, every morning this week. Is that correct?

Subordinate (S): Yes. I'm very sorry.

B: Tell me why were you late?

S: Well, the traffic's been very bad.

B: But the traffic's always bad, and you normally come to work on time. So, what's the problem?

S: Well … My mother's very poorly.

B: I'm sorry to hear that John. It must be very tough for you, as you are very close to your mother.

S: Yes, Alex, it's tough all right.

B: [*Pause.*] 'But, I don't see why you are late, John.

S: Well, mother now needs our full-time care. She can't be left on her own for a minute. Barbara, my wife, works nights and doesn't get back home until half-past eight. I immediately set off for work, but because of the traffic, I'm late.

B: I see. And because you want to get home as soon as possible to relieve Barbara, who must be tired out, you have left work at the normal time, rather than making the time up?

S: Yes and no, Alex. I have left at the normal time, but I have cut my lunch time to half-an-hour, and made up the time that way.

B: I see. I've no problem with that at all.

Solving a problem

The final example accentuates only the positive—and is factual.

The Alaskan Electricity Company faced terrible problems a few years ago. It managed over 1000 miles of overground telegraph poles, supplying electricity to a sparse and widely scattered population in very hostile weather conditions. As a result of the terrible weather, ice and snow gathered on the overhead cables, which frequently snapped under the weight. Teams of men had to travel miles to repair these cables. The costs of such operations exhausted all their profits.

EXAMPLE

The company solved the problem through a group of people questioning effectively. These are the questions:

'Why don't we shake the poles?'

'But that would be difficult with over 1000 miles of poles—but let's develop the theme.'

'OK. Why don't we get bears to shake the poles?'

'Well, yes, … but how can we persuade the bears to shake the poles? How can we motivate the bears?'

'Well, why don't we put meat on top of the poles? In their attempts to reach the top of the poles to eat the meat, they will shake the poles and dislodge the ice and snow.'

'But how do we get meat to the top of the poles?'

'I know, why don't we use helicopters to fly the meat to the poles and place it on top for the bears?'

'I have a better idea. Why don't we use the helicopters to remove the ice and snow with their whirring blades and forget about the bears?'

And that is what the Alaskan Electricity Company did—with considerable cost saving.

What works and why

Now let's look back at the conversations and problem and consider the primary reason why some conversations were effective and others were not. The effective conversations used OPEN questions as opposed to CLOSED questions.

As Rudyard Kipling wrote:

> *I keep six honest serving-men*
> *(They taught me all I knew);*
> *Their names were What and Why and When,*
> *And How and Where and Who.*

The difference between open and closed questions is explained diagrammatically in Figure 1.1.

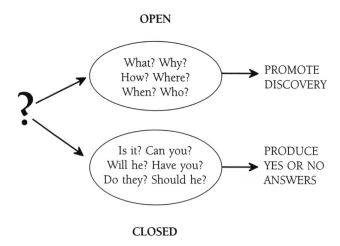

Figure 1.1 *Open and closed questions.*

We all, with rare exception, have a tendency to ask closed questions, for three key reasons:

1. *Our education*   Our schooling is much more about finding answers—being provided with information from which we develop conclusions—than it is about promoting discovery. As a result we have an inevitable bias towards questions that provide answers.

2. *Psychology*   One great advantage of closed questions is that there are immediate answers. We know subconsciously that by asking a closed question, we are guaranteeing that we shall have an answer. This means that outcomes are certain and controlled. Most of us like to be in control, and even if we do not, we like a degree of certainty. With open questions, there is an unpredictability of outcomes, generating uncertainty and we could lose control of the conversation.

3. *Ignorance*   Few of us are taught about open questions, and, for that matter, the full range and types of questions, which will be covered in Chapter 3.

Let's look at the examples.

■ Tim asked his boss one open question and that was it. As regards his subordinate, he simply told him—no questions at all. John, on the other hand, asked his boss two open questions and a closed one. With his subordinate, he asked nine open questions and a closed one.

■ The mother in the 'ineffective' case asked an open question, followed by a closed one, which ended the conversation. In the 'effective' situation, the mother asked five open questions and a closed one.

■ With the boss and subordinate in the 'ineffective' situation, the boss only asked closed questions. In the 'effective' conversation, the boss asked three open questions and two closed.

■ All of the eight questions in the problem situation were open.

Now there's much more to effective questioning than simply trying to ask lots of open questions. There is the type and nature of open and closed question; there is timing and mix, style and approach—all of which will be explored in later chapters.

To end this chapter, we shall consider the impact of questioning on relationships. Assuming that Tim and John did different jobs but each was a subordinate or direct report to the managing director, which do you think the managing director respected and valued more?

This is intended as a rhetorical question!

The managing director tended to tread on Tim, because Tim allowed that to happen. The MD's attitude towards John was more respectful—they had a better relationship because of John's approach.

I have met many bosses who have a number of direct reports and can get on badly with one and well with another. Many of the followers have not realized that the key determinant of the quality of their relationship with their boss is not some concrete absolute qualities and personality traits of the boss, but the quality of the questions they ask in conversations with their boss.

Similarly with parents, there are favoured and less favoured sons and daughters. How often has the compliant child been less well loved than the more assertive one?

If we teach our children how to ask us effective questions, we shall have better relationships with them. Equally, if we ask them the right questions, we shall also improve our relationships.

With partners, friends and even enemies, the same holds—I know of no exception.

What is the right context and approach?

What this chapter covers

In this chapter we look at the context of questioning—the structure of the conversations that build quality relationships. We also consider the right attitude and approach, and why, and conclude with the other side of the questioning coin—effective listening.

What is the right context?

If you refer to Figure 2.1, 'Questioning in context', you will see that the heading on the left-hand side is 'Issue'. Why?

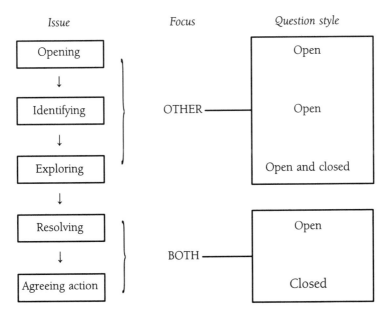

Figure 2.1 *Questioning in context.*

First of all, you may have noticed that all the conversations in the previous chapter dealt with an issue, if they were effective and successful. The issue with 'MD/manager/subordinate' arose because Charles was being moved from delivery into sales; the issue with 'mother and daughter' was that spotty Johnny was being sent to the headmaster; the issue with 'boss and subordinate' was the employee's lateness at work; and with the Alaskan Electricity Company the issue was the reduced profits, with work-teams repairing the overhead cables.

It is generally agreed that conversations that improve the quality of relationships are *conversations with a purpose*.

The purpose is to resolve an issue, solve a problem or seize an opportunity. Conversations without an explicit issue (a purpose) will drift around aimlessly or lead to a conclusion that is not desired by the questioner; they may even lead to breakdown as unexpected issues or problems of a negative nature can arise, and be 'resolved' negatively.

Furthermore, as all the conversations in the first chapter illustrated, *effective conversations are single-issue conversations*. There are two reasons for this:

1. To achieve anything in life, we need to focus. If we focus on one issue, we get optimum results.

2. Effective conversations require agreed action by both parties afterwards—the follow-up that maintains the momentum and gives both parties a sense of shared achievement. Again, if we ask ourselves and others to do too much, to commit to a number of actions by trying to deal with more than one issue, the probability is high (with the lack of focus and all the other pressures on our time) that either one or both parties will fail to do what was promised, thus reducing the quality of the relationship and achieving completely the wrong result.

Taking the mother/daughter example, the daughter is going to phone her friends to see how they can help spotty Johnny, and the mother is going to get home by 8 o'clock to receive a progress report, which is likely to lead to a further quality conversation.

We shall continue with this example when examining the flow suggested for effective conversations. The mother/daughter is a good example because there was no issue to start with and the conversation only became effective when an issue was identified through the skilful questioning by the mother. In the next chapter, we will consider the situation in which the issue is known.

Mother/daughter analysis

Opening (open)

This is the social opening, with an open question, usually how or what (we shall look in more detail at actual questions in the next chapter). In the case taken, it was: 'So how was school, dear?'. In the opening to a work-based conversation, it might be: 'So how was the traffic, Joanne?', 'So what time did you make it home last night?', 'So what sort of weekend did you have', and so on.

Identifying (open)

'So, what was the most exciting event of the day?' or, more generally, 'So why do you want to see me?', if it is someone dropping in, or 'How can I help you?' or 'What's bothering you?'.

Exploring (open and closed)

'Why was that?', 'Do you think that is a fair decision?' or 'What did she miss?'

Resolving (open)

'What do you think can be done about it?'

Agreeing action (closed)

Mother: I'll be back by 8 at the latest—so I'll see you then.
Daughter: OK Mum. I'll tell you what me mates say about seeing Miss Brown.
   Note: In this case, the closed question 'Is that OK/Agreed?' is implicit. With business relationships, it is useful to get verbal confirmation to agreed action.

What is the best attitude and approach?

We should understand not only the context of our questioning, but also the best attitude and approach, as well as the choices we need to make. If we look at Figure 2.1 under 'focus', we see that for a significant part of the process we need to focus on the person to whom we are talking, while only in the later stages can we bring our own position into play. This is a requirement if we are going to have effective conversations.

In all the effective conversations in Chapter 1, the focus was on the other person.

The exceptions are where our rights are being violated or where we are reacting to an aggressive individual (dealt with in Chapter 4). Unless we develop the frame of mind in which we initially push our agendas away, and avoid those closed questions that will otherwise flow with a natural force that we cannot control, we are doomed to have an ineffective exchange that diminishes the quality of the relationship. We have to develop the right frame of mind and the right attitude before we can either ask the right question or listen effectively to the answers we receive. (Listening is discussed in the last section of this chapter.)

To help us develop the right attitude and approach, we need to recognize three things, i.e. we must develop the three mindsets of selection, time and respect.

We need to be selective

One of my favourite quotations was stated by Brian Pitman (chief executive of Lloyds TSB): 'Strategy means focus and hard choices.' As we know, we have to develop a strategy for effective questioning and listening, and part of that strategy is to focus on the other person and a single issue.

There are two difficult choices: we must consciously and deliberately choose to focus on the other person so that we ask the right question, and we must also decide with whom to have 'conversations with a purpose', and how often.

If we try to have effective conversations with all the people we know, each time we meet them, we shall be emotionally exhausted, stressed out of our minds, and have no time to sleep! We have to focus on the few people with whom, at a personal level, the relationship is important to us (partner, child, close friend) or where the relationship is important to our business performance (boss, subordinate, team-member, client or prospective client). Additionally, in any ongoing relationship, there is need for the superficial, ritual conversation. For example:

'Hi, Charles, did you have a nice weekend?'
'Yes thanks, and you, Pauline?'
'Not bad, at all. A bit parky this morning. Still spring's just round the corner—so we mustn't grumble.'
'Too true. See you.'
'Bye.'

Thank God for closed questions! And how do we feel if the ritual is disturbed by a colleague who has had a bad weekend and actually wants to talk about it? Also, time is money, and most of us are more and more stressed in our working lives. It is difficult to hold an effective conversation in such circumstances. As far as possible, we need to provide a time and a place for these conversations, and learn how to postpone or avoid without causing offence. It is better to have no conversation at all than one that is guaranteed to go badly.

We need to find time

Picking up on the last paragraph, effective conversations last longer than ineffective ones—the case with all the conversations that worked in Chapter 1. We have to recognize that we have to invest our valuable time to save time. Charles, being effectively persuaded by his manager to move into sales, will save that manager time in the long term (i.e. better performance, less problems to deal with and so on). The manager with the employee who is late will not have to deal with that matter again. The mother won't save time—but the relationship instead!

It is important to have such key conversations (in the business context) as part of a planned regular series—not on an ad hoc, impromptu basis. That way we shall be prepared to give the time it takes, and what is more, have prepared ourselves mentally to have the right attitude, framed our objectives and even thought up some of the key questions. As someone once said: 'Failing to plan is planning to fail.'

We need to respect the other person

We need to have convinced ourselves (if necessary) that the person we are talking to is someone we value and whose opinions and views we respect. This theme is developed in the next section—effective listening.

Effective listening

Unless we can listen actively and effectively, all our good questions will be ineffective, and so will the relationship! In this final section, we answer three key questions.

- Why is listening difficult?

- How can we identify poor listening?

- How can we become better listeners?

Why is listening difficult?

There are six reasons:

Talkers are rewarded

Most of us learned as babies that making a noise brought attention. As children, the noisiest and loudest often became the leaders and innovators of childhood games and activities. In formal education, those children who always answered questions and spoke clearly and distinctly were more favoured and praised.

In adult and business life, the pattern continues. Those who make the most noise often gain more attention than they or their opinions deserve.

Talkers are rewarded.

In the boss/employee 'ineffective' conversation, the boss was a talker who loved the sound of his own voice, and only asked closed questions.

We are more important

Sometimes we say to ourselves—though rarely at the conscious level—that we are more important than the person to whom we are talking. This is understandable, as we all need to build our self-esteem and one way is to feel superior to the individual with whom we are conversing. This reality can be reinforced if we have 'superior' status, whether we are the boss in the work situation or the parent at home. For some parents, there can be the lingering after-effects of an upbringing, where they were treated as children by their own parents according to the philosophy 'children should be seen, but not heard!'.

If we think we are more important, whether consciously or not, we shall not listen effectively.

We are more knowledgeable

'A little learning is a dangerous thing.' A lot of learning can be even more dangerous, when it come to listening. This is a variation of the perception of importance reason—but this time it is not the person to whom we are talking who is unimportant, it is what he or she has to say (the content) that is unimportant. We know more than he or she does, and say to ourselves, deep down: 'Those who know nothing, have nothing to say.' Innocence and ignorance can be the source of much creativity and subsequent knowledge. Many inventions have come into being because somebody did not know 'it couldn't be done' or did not accept 'this is the way we do things round here' and somebody else listened. However, most of us succumb individually and collectively to the 'new boy syndrome'.

'Until you have earned your spurs, proved your competence, you have nothing to say.'

We think faster than another speaks

This means that we have time available, which can be put to *good* use by concentrating and trying to fully comprehend what is being said to us, or to *bad* use by allowing distractions and our own thoughts to intrude.

We develop mindsets

From the moment of our birth, we enter an uncertain world, with a complexity and a dynamic we can never comprehend. We are therefore driven, whether consciously or not, to manage that uncertainty. Some of us are capable of tolerating, even enjoying, high levels of ambiguity and uncertainty, but for all of us there is a degree and intensity that is unbearable.

To enable us to cope, we create and confirm areas of certainty—beliefs, assumptions, attitudes and opinions that we do not consciously question. If we did, we would raise the level of uncertainty in our lives. We would be taking a risk, as we are unaware of our breaking-point.

The stronger our mindsets, which are likely to increase in this age of increasing uncertainty, the more we can only listen to ourselves. As suggested in the previous section, we need to carry out a conscious and deliberate act of control, before we can ask the right question and listen effectively to the answer.

We can be poor speakers

The fault does not always lie with the listener. We can be poor speakers. We can speak too quickly. We can send out too much information. We can send out veiled messages with unsuitable speech patterns or mixed messages using body language inconsistent with the words we speak.

The other person may make it difficult for us, but this is a key skill of an effective questioner—the ability to use the power of questions to ensure that the messages received are clear to us, and, in the process, clarifying them for the speaker!

How can we identify poor listening?

If we can identify poor listening in ourselves, we can improve. If we identify poor listening in others, we can rectify the situation. Not only should we listen effectively to the other person, but ensure that the messages we transmit are effectively picked up. Again this can be achieved with simple questions to ensure comprehension.

At the heart of poor listening is body language: the non-verbal signals transmitted, and the gestures we make or postures we assume. But language has also a part to play. There are six useful classifications.

Aggressive listening

There are two types: deliberate and accidental.

DELIBERATE

We don't want to listen, but we have been forced to listen because of, say, a direct, emotional request. We have responded aggressively. Our heart is not in it, and we feel resentful. We fold our arms, presenting a barrier to the receipt of information, have a stiff posture and tend to glare.

The only way to avoid deliberate, aggressive listening, is not to be aggressive! On a more practical level, we can deploy what I term the 'assertive pause'. If we receive a request we did not anticipate, we are automatically likely to respond emotionally. If we do not like the request the emotions will be negative, and in this case of a direct request, we shall fall into aggressive listening, rather than effective questioning and listening.

The trick is to remember to pause before replying and take a few deep breaths—known as 'breathing through the rib cage'. We normally breathe shallowly at the top of our throats, unless taking aerobic exercise. By breathing deeply we oxygenate our brains or 'clear our heads'. This enables us to think more clearly, to control the immediate negative emotional reaction and to respond with effective questions and effective listening.

ACCIDENTAL

We feel we ought to be listening; we want to listen, but are not very skilled at 'active listening' and try too hard. We feel the need to reassure the other person verbally. 'Yes, I am listening to you!', which intimates to the other person that we are not! Our concentration at the conscious level makes us lean forward (perhaps invading the other person's body space unintentionally) with a stiff posture, and what we think is an interested look may be perceived as a discomforting stare!

The only way to avoid this 'non-conscious' type of aggressive listening is to practise at effective listening.

Passive listening

This is a very common form of poor listening! It occurs when we have no desire to speak, have resigned ourselves to listen (perhaps we are with a person who likes to hear the sound of his or her own voice) and we drift off, slumped in the chair, body half turned away from the speaker, hand over mouth to conceal the occasional yawn, and little eye contact as we tend to look elsewhere. If we seem to be drifting into this mode, we need to ask a probing, open question, such as: 'That's an interesting point, but how does it relate to the issue we are focusing on?' This is another reason to have conversations with a purpose; if we have established a purpose, we can then re-focus the speaker.

Listening interruptus

This occurs where we do not want to listen, we want to speak. In the early stages, assuming we cannot find an appropriate moment to interrupt, we are likely to fidget in some fashion, such as drumming our fingers or playing with a pencil (assuming that that is not the way we display nerves). Then we lean forward, and interrupt.

Often, both parties can be in this mode simultaneously. The result is a bewildering dance of never completed statements or themes, as the talking prize is snatched one from the other, and back again. The bodies move forward when talking and back as the threatened invasion of personal body space forces the involuntary move. The occasional fidget manifests itself if the unnatural state of silence is too prolonged!

The only way to avoid this is to develop the right mindset or attitude in advance of the conversation, and have the questioning skill to close down the verbiage of the other party.

Logical listening

This is where we listen with our minds, and not our hearts. We are deaf to the messages conveyed by the way the other person speaks the words, and the non-verbal signals provided. We hear and respond to the words only. 'I've got an headache' receives the reply, 'Then take an aspirin'.

Logical listening is often the precursor to passive listening. We start semi-detached because we are only operating at the logical and not the emotional level. We are quick with the obvious logical solutions, become bored and lapse into passive listening.

Logical listening can also be the precursor to aggressive listening. The speaker wants to share the feelings behind the verbal messages he or she makes, and is personally quite capable of working out the logical responses. The speaker picks up the lack of eye contact, and the lack of warm, supportive body language, which compounds his or her sense of irritation provided by the statement of the obvious. Assuming the conversation has not been terminated, he or she will often make the emotional appeal: 'You are just not listening to me.'

We shall then have the direct, emotional response (perceived negatively) that can trigger aggressive listening, in the absence of that 'assertive pause'.

Arrogant listening

When we feel very comfortable and confident, often in front of a subordinate, partner or child, we can adopt the posture of hands clasped behind our heads, leaning back, legs stretched forward or even on a desk (at work) or stool (at home), as we gaze at the ceiling or down our noses! It does not necessarily display arrogance when we are alone, as we could just be thinking. But it does if we are with another person, and are supposed to be listening.

It is a posture that many of us adopt, but resist recognizing that it has arrogant overtones. It is interesting to note how we automatically remove our feet from the desk, and change our stance, when the boss enters! In some oriental cultures, where the cult of the individual is less strong, it causes a personal affront if you display the soles of the feet to a business colleague or acquaintance.

This is a self-centred style of 'listening', based on an assumption of superiority, and is very passive as there is complete disinterest at both the logical and emotional levels. The body language is static, as the posture will be maintained whether we talk or listen. There is no positive eye contact, although we do not mind 'looking down our noses', which is the only way we can look in that position.

If our attention is eventually caught, then we will alter our postures and gestures, depending on whether we move into logical listening, aggressive listening, or listening interruptus. However, if we take that deep breath, and recognize what are we are doing and why, we can move into effective listening.

Nervous listening

We manifest this when we are in an awkward situation—a job interview, appraisal interview, talking to a 'difficult boss' or client, and so on. We want to listen and try to listen, but are only capable of listening to our heart-beat. This form of 'non-listening' manifests itself by nervous gestures, which are also displayed when we have to talk. There are almost an infinite number of nervous gestures, and each person has a favourite. We are seldom aware of making them. It is a matter of great surprise to managers, when they see themselves on video for the first time, to recognize this reality. We fiddle with our fingers, we fiddle with our hair, we fiddle with our faces, we cover our mouths and move the forefinger up and down our top lips, we tap-dance under the table, we move our chairs and tickle our ears. The list is endless.

As an aside, developing the ability to notice another's involuntary gestures, and hence nervousness, is a useful skill. If we want to generate empathy, we know we have a lot of work to do. If there has been verbal agreement to something we have said, we know that it was an involuntary agreement, unlikely to transfer into action.

Our nervous listening will also be conveyed by the fact that we ask information to be repeated because we have not heard it properly, or by giving the answer to the wrong question. As nervous listeners, there is little we can do, except take that deep breath or breaths to calm ourselves. When someone is behaving in this annoying manner, remember that it may well be nerves and try to calm that person down.

As a final point, we often try to control our nerves and gestures, and we partially succeed. Assuming we are sitting down, the gestures move to our feet (the tap-dance or shuffle), which cannot be seen. What a keen observer will notice is that we adopt a very rigid posture above the table.

How can we become better listeners?

There are seven key ways to becoming better listeners.

Be committed

We need to recognize and believe in the power of effective listening, that unless we listen effectively, we have wasted all those good questions—we have to want to listen 'actively'. 'Actively' is an excellent word, because it conveys the reality that we have to take a conscious act to listen well. As we now know, effective listening is not a passive thing, a meaning the word conveys, but a difficult skill in which we need to engage our hearts and minds actively if we are going to be effective and reap the rewards of our questions.

Be objective

We need to think, make that deliberate pause and take that deep breath. As we have seen, it is our feelings, our opinions, our prejudices (whether against the person or the content) or our nerves that deny us effective listening.

Just as good leaders learn how to take control, not of others, but of themselves, so too does the effective listener. At the beginning of a discussion, telling ourselves 'I am going to listen' will improve our listening skill. Our skill will also improve if we deliberately pause when that comment is made that will trigger an instant negative logical or emotional response. In short, we must be proactive, not reactive. Only when we have listened to ourselves can we listen effectively to another.

Suspend judgement

If we judge, we don't really listen. If we judge in the act of listening, there are two outcomes.

1. *We disagree* If we do not want to express our disagreement (boss, for instance), we shall be turned off and lapse into passive listening, thus denying an effective conversation. This passive listening can lead to the situation (which annoys so many bosses because they do not understand the reasons) in which we verbally commit to doing things we do not believe in or have no desire to do. We therefore do them badly, or not at all if we can find a good excuse!

   If we do express our disagreement, we shall move into aggressive listening, or listening interruptus, and our subsequent flow of closed questions will deny an effective conversation.

2. *We agree* That may seem fine, but early agreement will lose some little nuances or new angles that are lost because we have stopped listening.

Check for understanding

How often do both parties assume understanding, only to be rudely awakened subsequently by actions inconsistent with the understanding assumed. The phrase 'singing from the same hymn sheet' is now hackneyed, but we must regularly pause in the conversation to ensure mutual comprehension.

In the situation where we are giving a brief to another or a team—never, ever ask the closed question: Do you understand the task ... or brief ... or situation?

What do you think the reply will be, and why?

Invariably the answer will be 'yes', or a chorus of yesses, because people do not like to admit ignorance, or that they were not listening properly—especially if you are the boss. So ask an open question instead—a simple probing question: 'To make sure that everything is clear, can you please summarize the brief for me?' (which is a polite form of 'what is the brief?'). Then listen to the reply to ensure that nothing has been omitted.

In the normal situation, where you are doing the questioning, you would interrupt at a suitable moment. 'Let me recap to ensure that I understand the situation. Your boss has advised you that you will shortly be having an expanded role, that your team members don't yet know, that the changes may affect the size of the team, and you are worried about how you can handle the situation to maintain morale. What have I missed out?'

Notice the deliberate use of an open question, and not the closed 'Is that right?' or 'Have I missed anything out?'. With a closed approach, there is a natural tendency to say 'no' (reinforced if you have 'superior' status), because they are acknowledging that you have not got it right—have made an 'error'. With the open question, you are suggesting that you may have missed something out—so they are more likely to actually reflect on what you have said and tell you of any omission.

Use positive body language

The words we speak have only around 10 per cent of the total impact in face-to-face communication. The way we speak—the tones, modulation, intensity, phrasing and use of pauses—has around 35 per cent of total impact, and our body language—our gestures, posture and facial expression—has a highly significant 55 per cent.

If we are listening effectively, then we should display the right body language. If we consciously try to use the right body language, we shall probably feel awkward, but shall be better listeners: 'conscious incompetence' will lead with practice to 'conscious competence' and eventually to 'unconscious competence' or natural ability. 'Rubbish' I hear some of you say. Not at all. It is why people who are being trained in good telephone technique are told to smile. When they do, their tone of voice becomes warmer, and this is picked up by the listener. So let us consider facial expression, gestures and body posture.

FACIAL EXPRESSION

The facial expressions should reflect the feelings being expressed. If the other person is feeling sad, look sad; if happy, look happy; and if angry, look angry—angry together at the source of the speaker's anger.

If you are the source of the anger, that is a different situation. The speaker will receive the impression that you are angry with him or her, which is likely to be the case. This is the moment for the assertive pause, not the angry reponse. If no emotions are being expressed as the speaker is in logical mode, then look confident and thoughtful—you are both in thinking mode together. There should be fairly frequent eye-contact, but never a glare or stare. Such eye-contact stops you becoming distracted, and conveys the message that you are, in fact, all ears.

GESTURES

Gestures are for the speaker, not the listener. Through using appropriate gestures, the impact of the speaker's message is significantly enhanced. Gestures from the listener act as a distraction—a form of non-verbal interruption.

POSTURE

There is no single, correct posture, as the posture will vary according to the situation—the logic or emotion being expressed, the ebb and flow of the conversation. However, in all situations, an assertive posture should be adopted, not an aggressive or submissive one. For instance, when seated, the listener could take up an open position (neither legs nor arms folded), leaning forward slightly, with the head a little to one side, and hands clasped loosely together, resting on the lap.

There are variations, such as leaning back slightly (to accommodate the other person leaning forward), open posture, with one hand on the chin and the other supporting the elbow or sitting straight with legs slightly apart, each hand resting on the appropriate knee. This last position is the best position for the back, and is known as the Pharaoh's posture.

Another way of deciding an effective posture is to consciously avoid all the postures we have covered under poor listening!

Use words

An effective listener uses words in the right tone to convey the right meaning. There are two aspects: reflection and interest.

REFLECTION

As we have seen, we should use our faces to reflect the speaker's feelings. Equally, the words and tone can support this by paraphrasing the words or reflecting the feeling of the speaker. Let us look at two examples from Chapter 1:

> *Charles:* I'm not an aggressive, pushy type.
> *John* (his boss): No, you certainly are not.
> *Daughter:* We all feel very sorry for Johnny.
> *Mother:* Well, that does seem unfair.

INTEREST

Show interest by those little verbal noises or even words. The murmur 'mmmmhuh' (or variations, which I shall not try to spell) or 'Well, I never', 'You don't say' or simply 'I agree' (which John said twice in his conversation with Charles).

Appreciate silence

We tend to dislike silence, and rush in verbally to fill it. In fact, silence can be a very powerful way to uncover truth. At a judicious moment, when we have asked a searching question and received a short, unsatisfactory response, or we have made a telling statement, we fall silent until the other person speaks. What will often happen is that the other person will reveal what he or she has tried to conceal.

The person rushes in to fill that awkward pause, being very consciously concerned at the silence. The person is emotionally distracted, and what he or she was trying consciously to conceal slips out, or, at the very least, removes a veil, which, if we are listening effectively, we can pick up and probe.

However, this reality has more to do with effective interviewing skills (see Chapter 8) than with effective listening skills. The main point is that a natural discomfort with silence may often impair our effective listening, either because we do not pause to collect our thoughts and give a measured response (ask the right question), or we speak when it would have been better from the other person's point of view if we had remained silent.

We can, by being silent, give him or her time to control emotions or gather thoughts, or simply share together a pleasant mood or ambience. As Mozart said: 'Silence is the most profound sound in music.'

Finally, remember that just as poor listening destroys the power of the right question, without the right question you have little opportunity to listen effectively. The two skills are inextricably interlinked. If you want to improve the quality and effectiveness of all your key relationships, you have to develop both in tandem.

In Chapter 3, which is the final chapter of Part I, we look in more depth at 'What are the right questions?' and when and how they are used, as well as the 'dos' of effective questioning.

What are all the right questions?

What this chapter covers

We complete this part, 'What is the right question?', by looking at:

■ the difference between the two clusters of open questions: 'what, why, how' and 'who, when, where';

■ the difference between 'what', 'why' and 'how', and when to use them;

■ the 'dos' of effective questioning.

We use the examples from Chapter 1, build on the learning points from Chapter 2, and conclude with a conversation that resolves a real-life problem.

What is the difference between the two clusters?

If 'what, why, how' are the discovery kings, then 'who, when, where' are the action-planning queens. The first set are used mainly in the beginning and middle of the conversation, and the second set mainly at the end.

Effective conversations, as we have discovered, focus on the identification and exploration of a single issue, leading to action planning at the end. Effective conversations are part of an ongoing dialogue, each conversation punctuated by action by both parties before they meet again to progress the issue or discover a new issue and continue the building of a quality relationship, which yields mutual benefit in time and a long-term partnership over time.

So, at the end of such conversations, the following issues are determined: *who* is going to carry out the agreed actions, *when* the parties will carry out their agreed actions and *when* and *where* they will next meet.

The discovery kings

We now turn to an examination of the discovery kings: 'what', 'why' and 'how'. We start with 'what' as that is the king of kings or emperor of questions, as we shall see. I would draw your attention to Figure 3.1 'What does "what" do?'

What does 'what' do?

Identifies issues

OPEN
'What' can be completely open, as was the case with the mother and daughter—discovering the core issue, which will become the focus of the

- What should we talk about?
- What is the most interesting thing?
- What did you discuss at the meeting?
- What did you do yesterday?
- What have I missed or omitted?
- What questions should I ask?

- What is the problem?
- What is your vision?
- What is your objective?
- What is the decision?

- What would be the consequences?
- What do you mean precisely?
- What examples can you give?
- What situations did you face?
- What kind of people do you employ?

- What services do you provide?
- What are the facts?
- What books do you use?

Figure 3.1 *What does 'what' do?*

INVOLVES

- What is your view?
- What do you think?
- What decision do you favour?

REPLACES THE OTHER OPEN QUESTIONS

- What are the reasons behind?   = Why?
- What about?   = Why not?
- What methods/approaches did you use? = How?
- In what ways is it?   = How?
- What are your feelings?   = How do you feel?
- What time?   = When?
- What place?   = Where?
- What person?   = Who?

SUB-CLASSIFIES 'WHY'

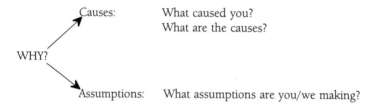

Causes: What caused you?
               What are the causes?

WHY?

Assumptions: What assumptions are you/we making?

Figure 3.1   *(continued)*

effective conversation. This is the case for the first four 'whats' under 'Open'. However, 'what' can also be used in the middle and the end. As we have discovered in the previous chapter, it is important that there is regular review or recap to ensure that you have completely understood the issue. At the end of such a review, the open question, 'What have I missed or omitted?' enables a sub-issue or key theme to be confirmed, which would otherwise be lost.

Additionally, it is very helpful to ask the previous question (appropriately paraphrased) towards the end of a business conversation. We shall use the codes Q for the questioner and A for the answer.

Q: Before we finish, Jane, is there any question I should have asked you that I have failed to?
A: Well, actually, I think you might like to know who else we are talking to? [... or whatever].

Note: This should never be asked as a substitute for previous good open questions, but in recognition that business people know their business better than you.

SPECIFIC

More often than not the issue is specific, and is established early on. In the first example in Chapter 1, the managing director had reached a decision—the reason for the meeting—and so the obvious question is 'What is the decision?'. A colleague approaches you with a problem, and you ask, 'And what exactly is the problem?'. 'What is your objective?' is another early question to ask, or perhaps 'Can we establish what the objective of this meeting is?'. We shall explore this in more detail in the skills development and relationship management sections.

I have included 'What is your vision?', because a motivating vision of the future is a core requirement for organizations in their attempts to manage change, and is a fundamental question we should ask ourselves on a regular basis. As someone once said: 'You cannot aim the rifle, unless you have a target.' Without a clear vision, at least 5 years hence and preferably 10, we shall be permanently in reactive mode rather than driving (through the development of a strategy, objective and actions derived from the vision) to achieve what will fulfil us.

There are so many people, particularly men, who fail to ask themselves this key question and die soon after retirement from work because they never created a vision of success beyond work, which would alter their focus of attention and activity during their final years.

Probes

'What' also probes, to enable the other person to think or to reveal facts. 'What do you mean precisely?' was used by John to probe Charles's thinking, when persuading him to move into a selling role.

Involves

'What' can involve the other person, and help develop the empathy that is at the heart of effective conversations.

REPLACES THE OTHER OPEN QUESTIONS

The reason why 'what' is the emperor of open questions is that it is the only question that has a unique identity, as the scene setting or identifying question. As the schedule shows, 'what' can also act as a substitute for all the other open questions, though most of the time we use them in their own right.

Sub-classifies 'why'

'What' enables 'why' to be probed or sub-classified. Let us take an example.

Q: Why did you shut the door?
A: Because I assumed that is what you wanted me to do.

OR

A: Because there was a draught.

We do things because there is some cause or because we make an assumption. By separating out 'why' into the causes or assumptions, we can probe both aspects. Probing assumptions is a key part of developing creative thinking skills, covered in Chapter 5.

What does 'why' do?

Please refer to Figure 3.2, 'What does "why" do?'.

Asks for an explanation

UNCRITICALLY
Questions like 'Why do we exist?' or 'Why did he do that?' ask for an explanation in an uncritical way and will cause no offence as they are impersonal.

CRITICALLY
As soon as we ask individuals to explain their behaviour, it can be taken by them as a criticism, whether intended as such by us or not. To avoid this, we should use a neutral, query tone of voice and positive body language, and, if we have not yet developed any empathy in the conversation, paraphrase 'why' with softer approaches, such as:

- 'It would help me understand the situation better, if you would give me your reasons for doing this?'

- 'That's an interesting suggestion. Tell me why do you think it is the best way forward.'

- 'So, please tell me the assumptions you made, when you did that.'

Determines causes

A sequence of 'whys' determines cause or causes from a series of effects. So taking the effect that sales revenues have fallen, one of many possible

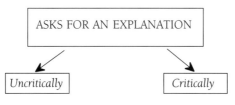

ASKS FOR AN EXPLANATION

Uncritically

- Why do we exist?
- Why did he do that?
- Why did she leave so abruptly?

Critically

- Why did you do that?
- Why did you make that assumption?
- Why did you fail to get authority?

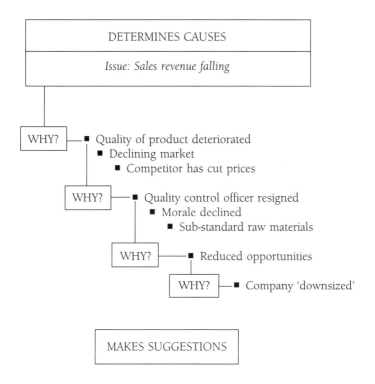

DETERMINES CAUSES

Issue: Sales revenue falling

WHY? — ■ Quality of product deteriorated
- Declining market
- Competitor has cut prices

WHY? — ■ Quality control officer resigned
- Morale declined
- Sub-standard raw materials

WHY? — ■ Reduced opportunities

WHY? — ■ Company 'downsized'

MAKES SUGGESTIONS

- Why don't we introduce reverse appraisal?
- Why don't you shut the door?
- Why don't we get bears to shake the poles?
- Why not introduce feedback meetings with your staff?

INVOLVES

- Why do you think this happened?

Figure 3.2   *What does 'why' do?*

causes is that the quality of the product has deteriorated. However, a cause is still an effect, if reasons can be provided to explain why it happened. So, one of many possible causes of a reduction in quality could be that the quality controller had resigned. One of the many possible causes of this could be 'reduced opportunities' and the direct and single cause of this was the downsizing of the organization.

Thus, a series of logic chains are produced, which will interlink, as some may lead to a single cause. Data may be required to determine the actual causes. However, as covered in Chapter 5, 'How to become more creative', this cause and effect analysis is a very powerful way of finding the real problem that needs to be addressed. Too often we deal with an effect and not with the cause, and tend to make things worse rather than better.

The reverse side of the 'effect' and 'cause' analysis using 'why', is to take an effect—a decision contemplated—and use 'what' to draw out the consequences, which is a key component of being an effective strategic thinker. This enables strategies to be evolved (a) to mitigate negative consequences in advance, (b) to modify the decision or in fact to rescind it, or (c) to change the decision-making process.

Makes suggestions

We use 'why' with a negative 'why don't ... ' or 'why not ... ' to introduce ideas. This aspect is developed in Chapter 5.

Involves

'Why' like 'what', can be used to involve the other person and develop empathy.

What does 'how' do?

'How' (see Figure 3.3) achieves five functions:

Asks for ideas

'How' initiates the search for ideas—i.e. it triggers discovery.

Probes thinking

'How' probes the thinking of the other person: 'How did you make a sale?' or 'How did you demonstrate supportive leadership?'

You may recall that 'what' also probes thinking, but there is a difference. The 'probing what' occurs before the 'probing how'. 'Probing what'

```
┌─────────────────────────┐
│     ASKS FOR IDEAS      │
└─────────────────────────┘
```

- How can we motivate the bears?
- How can we increase morale?

```
┌─────────────────────┐
│   Probes thinking   │
└─────────────────────┘
```

- How do you make a sale?
- How do you demonstrate supportive leadership?

```
┌─────────────────┐
│    Involves     │
└─────────────────┘
```

- How are you feeling?
- How would you tackle the problem?
- How do you do?

```
┌───────────────────────────┐
│ Establishes numerical facts │
└───────────────────────────┘
```

- How old are you?
- How often do you hold team meetings?
- How many staff report to you?

```
┌─────────────────────┐
│  Establishes price  │
└─────────────────────┘
```

- How much?

Figure 3.3 *What does 'how' do?*

identifies sub-themes flowing from the main issue, and if followed by 'probing how' enables a greater focus and exploration of that sub-issue. As an example, let us assume that the main issue is a proposed takeover.

Q: So what do you see as the consequences of the takeover?
A: Well, firstly, there will be inevitable rationalization. For starters, we shall only need one, streamlined, head office, which will mean some significant staff cuts and the potential of a severe loss of morale!
Q: And how can you ensure damage limitation?

Involves

'How' involves the other person, as do all the 'Discovery' kings.

Establishes numerical facts

This is mainly used for information gathering; e.g. 'How old are you?' or 'How many ... ?'.

Establishes price

The $64,000 question!

Turning now to the sequence of open questions, the generic format is mainly 'what' to uncover the issue, 'how' to promote ideas, 'why not' to make suggestions, finishing with 'what' for actions, 'who' for responsibility and 'when' for timing. The example at the end of the chapter demonstrates this sequence.

The 'dos' of effective questioning

In this section, we cover the key things we should do to ensure that we 'ask the right question'.

Think first

Where the time, place and person for a 'conversation with a purpose' is known in advance, as is often the case, the more we think and plan the conversation, the more effective it will be. Additionally, during conversations, as suggested in Chapter 2, use the 'assertive pause' to ensure that we remain in control of ourselves and, hence, the questions we ask.

Think open question

I was recently facilitating a practical session to help develop effective questioning skills in four managers employed by one of our clients. In our system, one manager states a real problem he or she wishes to discuss, another asks open questions in order to fully understand the problem, and the other two, and I, assume observer roles during the questioning and provide feedback.

In one case, the questioner asked an open question, followed by 14 closed—ending up pushing a solution to a problem he did not understand, much to the dissatisfaction of his 'client'. While this is extreme, the general norm, as we have established, is that we find it difficult to ask the right question, and we must therefore consciously think of the right open question to ask.

For instance, as we have seen, when recapping, we should not summarize and then ask the closed question 'Am I right?', but should ask 'What have I omitted?'. When establishing facts, it is much better to adopt the open route rather than state the facts and ask 'Do you agree?'. We should begin with the statement, 'Let us establish the facts'; and when all the evidence has been stated, continue with 'And let us think of any information we may have overlooked' before getting the closed agreement.

With this particular client, I have been involved in such practice sessions with scores of managers. There is one that I can recall particularly in which the questioner (in roughly a 10-minute period) asked only four questions, each open and probing, listened intently to the reply and then summarized the problem succinctly at the end. The 'problem holder' was surprised and delighted that the questioner had got to the heart of the matter; the problem had changed from the start—the right questions had lead to the right answer in this case, a shared understanding of the real problem.

Avoid leading questions

Leading questions can be phrased in a closed or open style, and are the antithesis to promoting discovery or even problem solving as they push or lead to the 'one right' answer.

- 'The chairman thinks we should sack Jones. What do you think?'

- 'Surely you do not have any doubts about our new mission?'

A variation is the *loaded* question. With a leading question, our own views are implicit; in a loaded question, they are explicit or loaded in.

- 'Do you not agree that John has poor time-keeping?'

- 'Why don't you drop dead!?'

Not a very open question!

Avoid 'logical' closed alternatives

Let us say the issue under discussion is 'a drop in sales'.

- 'Well clearly we have to either reduce costs or increase revenue. Which do you favour?'

In this situation it is better to take the open route: 'Let us consider all the options we could take to reverse this trend' or, even better, 'Let us think of all the possible causes of this problem'. After all, for all we know, the root cause could be demotivation of staff (which come from pursuing the options route) or the first signs of a market moving into decline, which may require a new strategy, like diversification, which might come from taking the causal route.

As both possibilities could only emerge from 'thinking causes', this little aside confirms a basic point made earlier. The starting point is to identify the real issue or root cause, and not solve what might be a symptom or effect. Incidentally, 'or' can be used exclusively, as in the above case (although there is no reason why you could not do both) or conjunctively, i.e. both alternatives can be selected. This should also be avoided.

Q: Did you go to the cinema or the theatre?
A: Yes!

Use perceptive probing questions

A perceptive probing question is one that you can only ask when you have become a good listener.

When you ask good open questions, the addressees open up—that is the purpose of the questions. In the course of answering particular questions, the addressees almost invariably drop in a phrase or even a sentence that is significant. This is inevitable as you are getting them to think—either to reveal what was hidden from you or to reveal what was latent or subconscious (hidden from them) or produce completely new thoughts.

If you are listening acutely, you can easily pick up this phrase, as there will be slight change in tone of voice or even body language.

Let us take the example of the manager who asked one open and fourteen closed questions of the 'problem holder' The problem as originally stated was that the 'problem holder' was a leader of a number of teams, each of which had a team leader, one of whom had resigned. He had complete autonomy as to what action he took, and he had to decide whether to hire a new team leader, promote from within the existing team (downsizing) or promote from within and hire a new team member.

First of all, he over-stressed the work 'autonomy'. No one in business has complete autonomy in present circumstances, and he had a boss who would have some views that he needed to ascertain, but that was not mentioned.

Next, although the questioner asked all these closed questions, the 'problem holder' responded as if they were open, because he was so anxious to air this real, important, work-related problem. On three occasions he dropped these little clues, left unprobed.

1. On the first occasion, he referred during a series of statements to the fact that he would have a 'bigger job', which should have been picked up and probed:

   ■ That's interesting. I noticed you mentioned that you would be taking on a bigger job? In what ways will your job become bigger?

2. On the second occasion, he dropped in the phrase 'moving away', which should have led to three open questions:

   ■ 'Thanks for that.' 'You mentioned that you would be moving away.' 'Where will you be going?' and after the reply: 'When will you be going?' and after that reply: 'And what will be the impact on your teams?'

3. Funnily enough, the third occasion was the *cri de coeur*. The 'problem holder' referred in the midst of other issues and points to 'how he could keep his staff motivated'.

My job was not to explore the problem but to facilitate feedback on the effectiveness of the questioner. My own view was that the real problem—which would have been uncovered with effective questioning—was: 'How do I keep my teams motivated, when I am going to take on additional responsibilities and be physically separate from them?'

The initial problem was only part of the bigger problem to be uncovered and would form part of the solution to that 'single issue' that could have led to an effective conversation. Part of the series of actions would have been a dialogue with his boss to obtain some guidance and support.

Use the right wording

The way the question is worded will have a major impact on the answer. This has been an implicit point before, but needs to be made explicitly. The general rule is to focus the question in order to focus the other person. Therefore, as examples:

- 'What do you mean precisely?' is better than 'What do you mean?', which could lead to 'I mean what I say'.

- 'In what ways is the job bigger?' is better than 'How much bigger is the job?', which could lead to 'Much, much bigger!'.

- 'What are all the possible actions we can take to reduce absenteeism' is better than 'How do we reduce absenteeism?' or 'What could all the possible reasons be for sales falling?' rather than 'Why have sales fallen?'. Both the former increase the probability of a wider spectrum of ideas (see Chapter 5, 'How to become more creative').

Keep questions simple

On a video, we have a persuasion role-play between two managers, where one took more than 10 minutes to ask his question. You should have seen the body language of the listener! If we are not confident, or we are too involved, or we are too rushed and speak before we think, we can get lost. We can start a question, go on a gentle ramble or lecture tour, recover, and revert back to the question in hand.

This is to be avoided, as it makes us look silly and puts the listener to sleep! We must keep our questions simple and to the point.

Keep questions single

A golden rule of effective questioning is 'one at a time'. More than one question can lead to confusion or evasion. The respondent can select which one to answer, and the others can be lost in the subsequent discussion.

A classic example of this occurred a few years ago, when a back-bench Labour MP put forward written questions, intended to embarrass the government by showing the extent of sex discrimination in the Civil Service. Not only did he ask multiple questions, but ended by asking whether male staff or female staff were in the majority!

The junior minister's written reply to the entire set of questions was one word: Yes!

Provide answers, when asked

There can be a danger that we get into an exclusive open question mindset, and always end up answering a question with a question! Sharing your experience and giving your opinion is a vital part of a leadership role and of any effective conversation. Often people lack confidence and need guidance and support. The trick is to try to build up confidence, promote discovery and develop thinking. Place the problem monkey back on the shoulders where it should rightly rest—by asking all the right open questions. However, if and when you are asked for your opinion or your experience, then freely give it. The point is not to impose it early on, but to pull first and push later (if asked). Too often, we simply push with all those closed, leading, logical alternative questions—and there is no real dialogue.

Practice

As said before, being an effective questioner (and listener) does not come naturally to most people. The only way you will improve is to practise, practise and practise again.

Concluding conversation

We shall take the problem mentioned when looking at 'perceptive probing', and assume the 'problem holder' is Brian, and the questioner is Jane, a friend, partner or colleague, who is genuinely interested in helping Brian with his problem. I have made a few points in brackets, where relevant.

Jane: So what's the problem, Brian?

Brian: Well, Jane, it's like this. I am in charge of four teams, each with a team leader, and one of my team leaders has resigned. So I have to choose, as I see it, between recruiting a new team leader, promoting from the team without replacement, or promoting from within and recruiting a new team member. I have complete autonomy as to the decision I make.

Jane: That's interesting. It's rare these days to have complete autonomy. What did your boss advise?

[Using 'what' enables the questioner to proffer advice by way of assumption that won't cause offence. It is sensible with major decisions to seek the advice/support of your boss, as will be covered in Chapter 9. If the 'problem holder' had not done so—which is unlikely in this case—then the open questions suggest that he should in a non-controversial way. So, if the boss's advice had not been sought, the conversation might proceed as:

Brian: *Well, actually, I haven't talked to my boss about this. Do you think I should?*

Jane: *Well, I think it is a good idea with important decisions to talk to your boss so that you can find out what her views are, and, if she agrees with you, at least she is in the know and will support you. What do you think?*

This is much better than a closed approach.

Jane: *Have you talked to your boss?*
Brian: *No.*
Jane: *Well, don't you think you should?]*

Brian: 'Well, reading between the lines, I think that she would like me to go the route of minimum expenditure—promote from the team and don't replace. To be fair to her, she did say that if I thought it necessary, she would support recruitment.

Jane: So—if you do decide to recruit, you will have to make a good case?
Brian: Absolutely.

[Pause.]

Jane: Well, before we consider the pros and cons of each option, tell me what other changes are taking place that could impact on your decision?

[Probing, and assuming—as is almost inevitable in a world of change—that there will be a bigger picture to the problem than that initially provided. This question unlocks the real problem. If it is answered in the negative, no harm is done, the core issue is confirmed as the original problem and the conversation can proceed to solutions and actions.]

Brian: Funny you should ask that—but there are a couple of changes that muddy the water. First of all, I am taking on a bigger job, and, secondly, I am on the move.

Jane: I see. Looking at the job first, in what ways will it be bigger?

Brian: Well, I am taking on a new team in addition to my existing team. This team is situated 50 miles from where I work now.

Jane: And that is where you are moving?

Brian: Yes—in three months.

Jane: I see—and what do you think will be the impact on your existing teams?

Brian: Well—all the problems of managing at a distance. We have an excellent team spirit among the team leaders and myself, and that will take a nose-dive, because we won't see so much of each other; it will be much more difficult for me to stay in touch with developments, help solve problems and so on.

Jane: Let's pause for a moment and see if I understand the situation. The core issue is how to keep your team leaders motivated and the teams effective, given that you will be physically absent and have to allocate chunks of time to handle your additional team responsibilities. What have I missed?

Brian: Well, nothing really, as the replacement issue is part of the overall problem we have agreed.

Jane: Good. So how can we solve the problem—what do you think you can do about it?

Brian: Well, that's a tricky one. One thing's for sure. I shall have to recruit a new team leader. No one in the existing teams is ready for promotion, nor is the timing right, and it would not be on to leave one team short-staffed, with the problems the teams face with my departure. I need all the resources I can get. But what else to do, I don't know. Have you any ideas, Jane?

[*Interesting, when the core issue is the 'bigger picture'—the more strategic issue, then the original problem can quickly be solved. Vision provides focus for action.*]

[*Pause.*]

Jane: Well, I think so. What about an on-site co-ordinator?

Brian: What do you mean precisely?

Jane: Well, have one of your team leaders take on the role of co-ordinator of the teams when you are not there—and report regularly to you between the meetings you are able to hold.

Brian: Yes—that's an interesting proposition—but what about putting the noses of the other team leaders out of joint? [*Pause.*] I think I have it—

rotate the role among all the team leaders, so each has it for three months of the year. I think we've cracked it.

Jane: So, what do you need to do?

Brian: Well, get onto Personnel straightaway, so that we start the recruitment process. With a bit of luck, we can get a good internal candidate in place within three months. Then tell my team-leaders of my new role, and what I propose to do both on the co-ordinating front and the replacement front—and get some feedback.

Jane: And what should you do first of all, putting a political hat on?

[*A little bit of gentle steering.*]

Brian: Ah! yes—early meeting with the boss to get her agreement and make the case for the replacement, then onto Personnel and then the team meeting.

Jane: And when do you think you can do these?

Brian: No problem. I shall talk to my boss tomorrow morning, telephone Personnel in the afternoon and tell my team members at the regular meeting next Monday.

Jane: Good. So how do you feel about things now?

Brian: A damn sight better than before we had this chat. Thanks a lot for all your help, Jane—much appreciated.

Conclusion

The sequence of questions was 'what', 'what', 'what', 'how' (phrased using: in what ways?), 'where', 'what', 'what' (these uncovered the core issue), 'how', 'why not' (phrased using: what about?), 'what', 'what', 'when', and an ' "involving" how'. The emperor king was much in use. Probing using 'what' to uncover the real issue took up most of the conversation before 'how', 'why not', 'what', 'what' and 'when'. The 'who' was obvious in this conversation, which did not lead to mutual action, as Jane was in an adviser/helper role.

Effective conversations always have a discovery element, due to the quality of the questioning and listening skills of at least one party. Through Jane's gentle probing as well as helpful advice, both parties contributed to the positive outcome, which was discovered during the conversation.

Part II
HOW TO DEVELOP KEY SKILLS

How to become more assertive

What this chapter covers

In this chapter, we look at what assertiveness means, and how it is important to respect another's rights at the same time as asserting our own, except in the rare situation where the continuation of the relationship is unimportant. We take specific real-life situations and conversations to demonstrate how individuals have been effectively assertive, and analyse the questioning approaches that produced success. We finish with outlining an assertive code, which can be followed in the work situation.

What assertiveness means

There is a spectrum of views on assertiveness, with the starting point coming from the dictionary definition of 'insistence on a right or opinion'—a rather aggressive definition! A more positive, but still one-sided, definition is 'the positive, honest statement of our feelings, wants or desires of other people'.

However, when managers have learned and practised this self-centred form of assertiveness and then go back into the workplace to implement it, they come unstuck, much to their surprise and annoyance. The reason is lack of mutuality in the approach. For effective assertiveness, we need to adopt an approach based on the recognition of a mutuality of rights or 'expressing oneself in such a way as to achieve and maintain an effective expression of the rights of both parties involved'.

When we are truly assertive, we stand up for our own rights and also recognize and stand up for the rights of the other party. We need to be proactive, though we are reacting (we can achieve this by using the assertive pause technique) and we need to understand the other person's point of view if our response is to be effective.

As in all effective conversations, the fundamental basis for assertive behaviour is mutual respect. This is based on self-respect, as otherwise we will be aggressive or submissive: aggressive, if we use conscious over-confidence and a desire to control to create certainty and to still that inner voice of doubt and darkness; submissive, if we look to others to provide what we know we cannot find in ourselves. It is also based on respect for others, without which we can only be aggressive. We empower ourselves and empower others. We make the submissive assertive. If we fail, we lapse into aggression. We make the aggressive assertive. If we fail, we lapse into aggression or submission.

We use effective questioning and listening to achieve the mutual goal.

This is why individuals versed in the 'my rights only' school failed. With a submissive person, they were perceived as aggressive; they may have imposed their will, but there was no quality relationship. With an aggressive person they found it impossible to impose their will and lapsed into aggression or submission. Finally, they annoyed the initially assertive person because of their emphasis on their rights, so that eventually the other party reacted by 'insisting on his or her rights' and mutual aggression resulted!

Now, with any rule there is an exception. We have referred to that in Chapter 2, page 16, when discussing attitude and approach. In those extreme workplace situations in which our rights are being violated and trampled underfoot, we focus on ourselves and use the assertive pause technique, powerful probing questions, and some 'righteous anger' to recover the situation or gain as much benefit as we possibly can.

We need a clear head, good questions and courage to be successful.

A word of warning. Such an approach is only appropriate if the situation faced means that we no longer need to have a relationship with whomsoever is doing the trampling. I shall provide an example of the need for a mutual approach on the section on 'How to achieve mutuality', when an employee was summoned by his chief executive officer (CEO) and told he was going to be sacked. He is still working for that company, and has recently been promoted—but only because, at that fateful moment, he achieved mutuality.

How to assert rights effectively

We shall now consider a specific situation and conversation, based on reality, which demonstrates how rights were effectively asserted.

CASE STUDY

The situation

A law firm was badly affected by the recession in the early 1990s, because it had too much property-based business, which went from boom to bust rapidly. Because of large, increasing losses, which had been concealed from the main body of the staff who were not partners of the firm, it was decided to sack a number of assistant fee earners. This would be a first for this firm. One such assistant—we shall call her Jenny—was asked by her partner or 'boss', George, to come to his office the morning after that decision. She had been in employment for just over a year, had had a good appraisal from George, and had been told she would receive an 8 per cent pay rise.

The first conversation in the morning was with George and the second, in the afternoon, was with Peter, the partner responsible for personnel matters. This firm did not have professional staff in the functional roles.

Jenny and George

Jenny: You wanted to see me George?
George: Yes, Jenny—do sit down. I am afraid I have some bad news for you.

Jenny said nothing

George: Er! yes ... I am afraid, em, ... that we are going to have to let you go.
Jenny [*pausing for a moment*]: What precisely do you mean?
George: I mean, em, what I say, Jenny—that we are having to let you go— dispense with your services, as it were.
Jenny: Why?
George [*mumbling*]: Em, ..., because your work is not up to scratch.
Jenny: What do you mean—not up to scratch! You have just given me an above average appraisal and an above average pay rise of 8 per cent. Are you saying that my work has deteriorated in the last fortnight, and, if so, what evidence have you?
George [*in acute embarrassment*]: Well, no, not at all. ... Oh! dear.

And George proceeded to walk out of his own office!

Jenny and Peter

In the afternoon, Peter telephoned Jenny and asked her to come to his office.

Peter: Do sit down, Jenny. I gather you had a bit of a run-in with George, this morning.
Jenny: A bit of a run-in! George told me I was going to be sacked, gave my incompetence as the reason, and when I pointed out that he just assessed me as highly competent, and where was the evidence, couldn't give a reply and walked out of his own office!
Peter: Ahem—yes, George could have handled matters a little bit better. But the point is that, most regrettably, we will have to let you go, and quite a few of your colleagues I am afraid. You see the thing is that, most regrettably, we have been making huge losses in the Property Department, and with the level of business that we are getting at the moment, we simply have to reduce our staff numbers. I am very, very sorry, Jenny—but that's the way it is.
Jenny: Well, I am not happy about this. I think I have been treated disgracefully. I don't want to bring in the Industrial Relations Tribunal, but I will have to

consider that option. By the way, what redundancy terms will you offer me?
Peter: Oh! Yes—redundancy terms. [*Pause.*] I tell you what, we will give you six months in lieu. Is that acceptable, Jenny?
Jenny: Yes, that's fine, thank you Peter.

Review

A few observations before we look at the questioning approach. Jenny was a very smart cookie. According to the law, as she had been employed for less than two years, she was not entitled to any redundancy payment! She walked out with over £20 000. True, she might have tried the Industrial Relations approach, but their top payout at the time was only £11 000, it is time consuming, and tends not to lead to good references (which she got) or to other firms employing her!

Incidentally, she recognized that the writing was on the wall, and so did not have to pay attention to her relationship with George or Peter. If George had remained her boss, he probably would not have forgiven her the embarrassment she had caused him. No doubt Peter, having made his generous offer out of a mixture of guilt at her treatment at the hands of George and the threat of the Industrial Relations Tribunal, would have eventually decided 'he had been tricked' and blamed Jenny. It did not matter—nor would have it concerned Jenny as she spent the money and six months travelling the world!

Her questioning approach (after the necessary assertive pause) was impeccable, and consisted entirely of open questions (we shall analyse them in the next section). She used righteous anger and a real threat (reluctantly!), and she set out the facts of the meeting with George without rubbing Peter's nose in them.

Questioning approach

Looking back we see:

1. What precisely do you mean? (Probing thinking.)

2. Why? (Determining cause.)

3. What do you mean? This looks as if it probes thinking—but was used rhetorically, i.e. to create an effect rather than ask for an answer. Here Jenny uses it forcefully to express disagreement with George's suggestion she is incompetent. She then moves on to provide the facts that support the case she makes that George is wrong. This rhetorical approach can be used with 'how'—e.g. How dare you say that?—followed by the facts that make the suggestion invalid. It can also be

used with 'why?'—'Why, ladies and gentlemen, have we put up with this for so long?'—followed by the reasons.

We should notice here the power of body language. The same question 'What do you mean?' if asked in a calm way with a slight query tone is a 'probing question', whereas if asked with a greater query tone, more intensity, modulated with a high pitch at the end, supported by strong, expressive body language—with a slight pause—it becomes a rhetorical question, to which we then proceed to give the answer.

4. What are the redundancy terms? (Probing facts.)

How to achieve mutuality

You will have noticed that Jenny's questioning was quite aggressive, which helped her achieve a good result from what appeared a hopeless cause. As she would have been made redundant whatever her approach, she did not need to worry about the impact of her questioning style on the listeners. That sort of reality is rare, and so, in most cases, it is vital that an attempt at a mutuality approach is made. Unless this is achieved, the relationship will suffer. Even if we win in the short term, we shall lose in the long term unless the other party feels happy about our approach and the outcome of the conversation.

Again we take a true story, describe the situation and conversation, then review the conversation and the questioning approach.

Late on a Friday afternoon, a consultant (Harry) working in a training consultancy receives a telephone call from his CEO (Cedric), asking him to come to his office.   **CASE STUDY**

Cedric: Sit down, Harry. I am afraid I have some bad news for you. As you know, the recession has and is continuing to hit us very hard, and we have to reduce staff numbers further than we had originally planned. So I have decided to let you go.

Harry [assertive pause—quite a few, in fact]: I appreciate that we are going through tough times at the moment, and you therefore have to take tough decisions. May I ask who else is being let go?'

Cedric: Only you, to be honest.

Harry: I see, and why have I been selected?

Cedric: Well, not to beat about the bush, Harry, and I don't want to upset your feelings—but I have to be honest. The truth is that you are the consultant with the worst performance record and the lowest utilization rate.

Harry [assertive pauses]: As you know, at your request, I moved nine months ago from training technologies to a consultant role—to save us money and increase revenue flows. Initially and inevitably, I got only just above average ratings from my clients. In the last two months my ratings have averaged over 5. [*They used a scale from 1 to 6 with the performance standard set at 4.5*]

Cedric: Oh! dear. John [*Harry's boss*] did not mention this. This is very encouraging news—but that does not alter the fact the you have the lowest utilization.

Harry: If we look at the last three months in my consultant role, and compare them to the first six months, then my utilization has more than doubled. The trend is in the right direction.

Cedric: Well, that's a fair point, I had not appreciated—but the absolute figure is still on the low side.

Harry: I accept that and I accept that it has to improve radically. May I suggest that I have meetings with John and Penny [*another key player*] with the view to developing a plan to build on my recent good performance—to increase both my use in delivery on other accounts as well as a strategy to increase my own accounts. Once this plan is in place and agreed with you, you can review my results on a regular basis to ensure I achieve accelerated progress to achieve full utilization.

Cedric: Well, let me see. It's not quite what I anticipated—but it seems fair to me. Give you another chance, eh Harry—why not. You deserve it, my boy. Best of luck.

A hearty hand-shake ensued, and Harry left in one piece, his mind in a turmoil, but his job intact.

Review

While Harry asserted his rights to keep his job on the back of good performance and improvement in utilization, he only did so because he avoided the aggressive questioning that Jenny adopted and explicitly and implicitly recognized the key rights of his boss's boss—the CEO.

Specifically, he explicitly acknowledged the CEO's right to make staff redundant by the powerful statement: 'I appreciate that we are going through tough times at the moment, and you therefore have to take tough decisions.' Notice the deliberate and empathetic use of we (not you), the reflection (another demonstration of empathy) and the acknowledgement of the role (and the difficulty of that role) of the CEO to take tough decisions (yet another demonstration of empathy). (The use of empathy in persuasion is discussed in Chapter 6.)

He implicitly acknowledged his CEO's right to make mistakes—i.e. not knowing that his performance had been good recently or that his utilization had dramatically improved. He did this by avoiding any 'righteous anger' at his CEO's ignorance. He also accepted that his utilization failed to meet the minimum target, having given a valid explanation.

Finally, he was proactive with a 'why not' suggestion to solve the problem, transferring the burden of action to where it rightly belonged—himself. Not all of us would have appreciated that reality!

Of the many, many stories of managers and others who have been fired, his is the only one I have encountered in which the situation was saved by an individual who knew how to achieve mutuality and avoid focusing on personal rights, perceived violated.

Questioning approach

Success was achieved by asking the right open question at the right time, and using facts to support his case, which was delivered in a calm, clear way. There were no closed questions (the effective questioner will very rarely use them) and three open ones:

1. May I ask who else is being let go? (Establishing facts.) This was the key question. If you have worked out the key question, always ask it first. It was key, because if the answer was 'Well, actually, we are letting three other consultants go', then Harry's goose was well and truly cooked—so he might as well focus on getting the best deal from the CEO. However, he was the only one.

   Another important point, mentioned in Chapter 2, is the actual content of the question. Harry knew that his CEO was a very reluctant sacker (some consultants had been 'let go' a year earlier, when the recession had first bit deeply), needed to be pushed into it and so would not like explicit reference to this fact provided by saying 'Who else are *you* letting go?'

2. Why have I been selected? (Asking for an explanation.) Notice that, again, Harry avoided the personalization 'Why have *you* selected me?'. (It would appear that Harry had a less than supportive boss, who might well have been prepared to sacrifice Harry and could even have been the force pushing the CEO into his reluctant decision.)

3. 'May I suggest'—a 'why not suggestion'. Harry had managed to listen effectively to his CEO (only possible because he had avoided the flood of closed, leading questions), had picked up on his own boss's lack of support, and so knew he had to meet formally with him to mend whatever fences were broken. Incidentally, he achieved this through powerful open questions and an empathetic approach, so that his boss moved from a very lukewarm position to being his champion in the organization. We look at the relationship with the boss in Chapter 9.

Before we finish with the mutuality code, I would point out that there is a commonality in assertive questioning, whether the rare insistence on rights or the more common drive for mutuality. Both require probing questions to establish facts and uncover reasons, and both require the delivery of facts to support a proposition made.

Both also require the need to control the immediate negative emotional response that sudden bad news will automatically generate by giving ourselves those vital few moments of 'heavy breathing'!

The mutuality code

I finish this chapter with this code, developed as a guide to those who want to follow the path of mutuality in the workplace.

- To respect myself and others.

- To make mistakes, admit them and to learn from them. To allow others to make mistakes and help them learn from them.

- To express my views and opinions and encourage others to do the same.

- To listen and be listened to.

- To say how I feel as well as think, and encourage others to do likewise.

- As a leader, to explicitly agree with my followers their job responsibilities, objectives, and performance standards. To help them achieve their objectives, and provide regular feedback on their performance. To discipline the follower when she or he has been provided with support and failed to meet agreed standards.

- As a follower, to ensure that I know and accept my responsibilities, objectives and performance standards; to work to the best of my ability; to know how my leader sees my performance; and to resist unreasonable requests that are not part of those agreed responsibilities.

- To learn to ask the right question!

How to become more creative

What this chapter covers

We can all be much more creative than we think we are. There are individuals who appear to be naturally creative and can run 800 metres effortlessly, yet, although we lesser mortals labour to complete a mere 100 metres, we all can run marathons. If we follow the right rules, 'ask the right questions' and use the right techniques, we can transform our ability to be creative.

I had a boss once, a Fellow of the Institute of Chartered Accountants, who saw himself, and was seen, as a very logical, precise and pragmatic type—not at all creative. By using the discovery technique in a team environment, he (and all the team members) became much more creative than any of them thought possible.

In this chapter, we look first at what exactly constitutes an idea, what are the golden rules that ensure discovery, what are the questions and question combinations that enable us to be more creative. We then consider two additional techniques (other than those covered by the question combinations) and conclude by looking at how to guarantee that a small group will be more creative than any individual.

What is an idea?

This may seem to be a strange question, but bear with me. In fact, with a pencil and paper jot down an area where there could be improvement, such as increasing sales in your organization, or any area you like. Having identified the area, write down a few ideas that will cause improvement.

If we take the example of sales and consider the question of how we could increase sales we could have:

■ Hire more salespeople

■ Cut the price of products or services

■ Spend more on training

■ Improve the morale of the salesforce.

Now let us look at these ideas. They are simply actions or action areas. Hiring more salespeople is an action, cutting the price of products or services is an action, spending more on training is an action and improving morale is an area where actions are required if morale is to be improved and sales increased.

So ideas are simply actions that need to be taken, or action areas where more ideas or alternative actions need to be developed. In fact, an idea is not effectively developed until it has been progressed into actions—hence the well-known phrase 'action planning'. There is rarely one right answer, as a single action is rarely likely to solve any problem of a non-technical nature. However, a series of actions, which are not mutually exclusive and are implemented over as long a time frame as possible, will enable effective change.

I remember how the Deputy Prime Minister in the UK, Michael Heseltine, when in charge of Transport, dismissed the suggestion of expanding the rail infrastructure as a way of solving road traffic congestion. He was right insofar as a single action could not have solved the problem. However, a series of actions, such as expanding the access and frequency of buses, providing penalties and incentives to reduce the use of the car, increasing passenger occupancy, expanding roads and rail freight and so on—including the expansion of the rail infrastructure—implemented as part of a 5- or even 10-year plan, would have reduced road traffic congestion.

A few other interesting points are worth mentioning at this stage.

Experts try to separate out logical and creative thinking and give creative thinking a mystique and a degree of difficulty that can, quite under-standably, put off logical pragmatic types. Think of the language 'brainstorming', 'conceptualization', 'blue sky thinking'!! How much more valuable and relevant is it to say to a group: 'Let's get together to think up alternative actions we need to take to solve the particular problem or issue we face!'

The more logical we are, the more creative we can be. I have always been taken by Edward de Bono's model of creative thinking. He postulates that the brain operates in stable thought patterns, and we tend to move logically from one stable state to a connected one. To have a good idea we need to provoke the brain from its comfortable path, suspend judgement and generate movement. Then, in a flash, the good idea comes to us—but is only recognized if we connect back logically to where we started. So we cannot generate ideas by logical foresight, but will only recognize a good idea in logical hindsight. There is a complete analogy with humour. We do not understand the comedian until the punchline—the illogicality—but only laugh if we can connect back logically. If we do not, we say: 'I don't understand that.'

So the more humour we generate, and the more logical we are, the more ideas we shall have—provided we suspend judgement. That's the difficult bit, because the more logical we are, the greater has our critical faculty been developed, which brings us neatly to the two golden rules of being creative.

What are the two golden rules?

These two (connected) rules apply whether we are on our own trying to think of some ideas, and particularly where a small group of us are thinking creatively.

1. *Exploration should be separate from and followed by development, which should be separate from and followed by evaluation.*

2. *There must be no criticism by word or body language during the exploration and development phases.*

Look at the second rule first: if there is criticism (part of evaluation) when someone makes a suggestion, that will very effectively stop that individual (even if it is us criticizing ourselves) making another. In fact, if that individual is the first to be criticized in a 'team' situation where the leader has been the source of the criticism, then all the team members will rapidly respond with no further ideas, leaving the field open to the leader, who then suggests the 'one right answer'. I have seen it many, many times.

If the logic of criticism had been applied to the Alaskan situation at any time, the ultimate solution could never have been found. For instance: 'Don't be ridiculous, there are over 1000 miles of poles, far too many to be shaken!' or 'It just won't work. Research indicates that there are only 100 bears, far too few to shake the poles. In any case, with respect, the suggestion that bears would shake telegraph poles is far too fanciful' and so on.

Body language must not be ignored—the accidental or deliberate hostile response by look or body movement can be just as effective as words.

It follows that if criticism destroys creativity and must not be allowed, then exploration (and development) needs to be separated from evaluation or criticism. The need for the second rule determines the first.

There also needs to be a development process after the exploration process. When we have an initial set of ideas, many may well be simply action areas (as was the case with 'Improving morale of sales staff') which will need to be developed into alternative actions.

Use specific question combinations to be creative

We look at five question combinations that will enable us to be more creative: why/why, how/how, why not/how, whats/hows and what/why.

Why/why

We have seen this combination before, when looking at the uses of 'why' in Chapter 3—determining causes (see Figure 3.2 on page 33). I draw your attention to Figure 5.1, which has much in common with the 'determining causes' slide. There are two key points to make:

1. As stated in Chapter 3, the actual phrasing of the question is important. We would not use a bald 'why', but the more open question, 'What could all the possible reasons be for' followed by the issue or problem under consideration. We need to encourage what is termed 'thinking outside the box'—i.e. breaking free of the usual assumptions and mindsets we all develop—and consider new insights and angles. This is permitted, nay desirable, in the exploration phase.

    So we phrase the question in this way to enable us and others to suggest all sorts of possibilities. This increases the probability that, as we develop each initial sub-issue with another 'What could all the possible reasons be for', we shall propose a set of reasons or causes that are more all-embracing than would otherwise be the case.

2. A cause is also a possible solution—either action area or alternative action. So, by following the 'why/why' approach, we are uncovering a set of solutions at the same time! Taking the example, and accepting that there could be a much wider range of causes at each level, let us

What could all the possible reasons be for:

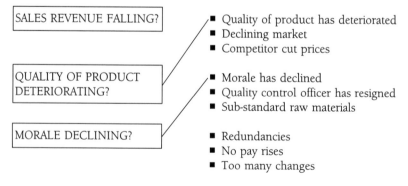

Figure 5.1   *Why/why.*

assume that the market is expanding and there has been no competitor price war. We then know that we need to improve the quality of the product to reverse the decline in sales. We already have a set of options to consider as a remedy, because we have followed the 'decline in sales' down the causal chain.

How/how

This is the traditional creative thinking route. I would draw your attention to Figure 5.2, and again make two points:

1. Rather than using the bland 'how', I suggest a question which focuses on action (the end product of creativity) as well as encouraging exploration: 'What are all the possible actions we could take to' followed by the area to be improved, in this case 'increase sales revenue'.

2. When we use 'What are all the possible actions we could take', we may well come up with more action areas rather than specific actions. So we apply the long version of the 'how', until it is obvious that it is no longer the right question—that, in fact, a different open question needs to be asked to achieve the detail required for implementation.

So, at the first level use, we have 'cut prices'—the end action area, as the question 'What are all the possible actions we could take to cut prices?' is a nonsense question. However, for implementation or decision taking we

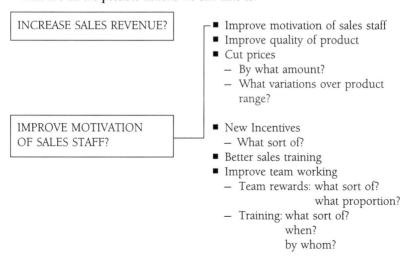

What are all the possible actions we can take to:

INCREASE SALES REVENUE?
- Improve motivation of sales staff
- Improve quality of product
- Cut prices
  - By what amount?
  - What variations over product range?

IMPROVE MOTIVATION OF SALES STAFF?
- New Incentives
  - What sort of?
- Better sales training
- Improve team working
  - Team rewards: what sort of? what proportion?
  - Training: what sort of? when? by whom?

Figure 5.2   *How/how.*

would need to ask different questions such as 'By what amount?' and 'What variations over product range?' In real life, research would be needed to determine what was the price cut for each product that maximized the increase in revenues.

Equally, at the first level, we have 'Improve motivation of sales staff'. As this is still an action area, we can apply the long-form 'how' question, and get a series of answers. This process continues until you have an action area, where a different type of question needs to be used. As shown, 'Training' is an action response to the question 'What are all the possible actions we could take to improve team working?' and the final questions to enable action planning or implementation are: 'What sort of?', 'When?' and 'By whom?'

Why not/how

We have already seen this combination in action with the Alaskan Electricity example, used to find a single action area from the root cause of the problem. The symptom was the hit on profits, caused by the cost of work-teams, addressing the root problem—ice and snow breaking the overhead cables. Recalling the sequence, we had:

- Why not shake the poles?
- How can we shake the poles?
- Why not use bears to shake the poles?
- How do we motivate the bears to shake the poles?
- Why not put meat on top of the poles?
- How do get meat to the top of the poles?
- Why not use helicopters to put the meat on top of the poles?
- Why not forget the bears, and use the helicopters to sweep away the ice and snow before it breaks the cables?

Similarly, if poor quality was the one cause of loss of sales revenue, a why not/how sequence could be:

- Why not improve the quality of the product?
- How can we do that?
- Why not ensure that staff are more committed to eradicating quality defects?
- How can we do that?
- Why don't we give them more responsibility and autonomy?
- How can we do that?

Why don't we develop self-managing teams, who are allowed to implement any quality improvements they determine to be relevant?

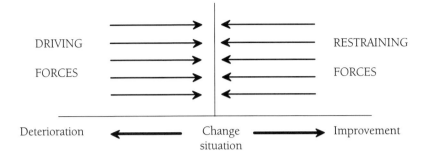

- What are all the possible driving/restraining forces?
- What are the priorities?
- What are all the possible actions we can take (how?) to reduce the impact of the key restraining forces/increase the impact of the key driving forces?

Figure 5.3 *Whats/hows: force field analysis.*

Whats/hows

I draw your attention to Figure 5.3. The technique is known as force field analysis, but like most creative thinking or problem-solving techniques, it boils down to open questions.

Any problem/change to be introduced or situation to be improved is the issue. As an example, we could take 'use of a networked system'. The current use would be a position of dynamic equilibrium, held in balance by the impact of two opposing forces—restraining forces and driving forces. The restraining forces push towards deterioration (i.e., in this case, less use of the system) and the driving forces push for improvement (i.e. greater use).

If the power of a single restraining force is reduced, or the power of a single driving force is increased, the balance point (in this case the degree of use) will shift in the improvement direction. Therefore, having identified the end goal over the time period, continuous improvement can be made to achieve it. The initial process, which can be repeated regularly, consists of a series of open questions and answers.

Step 1: Identify forces

What are all the possible driving forces (e.g. enthusiastic support staff, a champion, business need, customer demand, easy access and so on)? What are all the possible restraining forces (e.g. fear of technology, lack of databases, poor training, poor understanding of benefits, poor system co-ordination and so on)?

Step 2: Prioritize

What are the most important driving/restraining forces? As this can be used as a team tool, it is wise, at the first run, to limit yourself or the team to no more than two key driving forces/restraining forces, otherwise you will end up with too many things to do. In a team situation, the easiest way to prioritize is for each individual to select his or her top two, and use a scoring system to determine the two favourites.

Step 3: Action plan

Apply the how/how approach (but using the action phrasing) to develop action plans to reduce or eliminate the impact of the two key restraining forces, and to increase the effectiveness of the two key driving forces (or introduce one or two new driving forces, discovered in the initial exploration phase).

What/why

This is a simple and powerful technique that recognizes that we all make assumptions, some of which can be invalid. This fact came home to me forcefully only recently.

I have a neighbour, who is middle aged and overweight. To keep his weight in check, he runs a marathon each year and puts in some training before the event. I was talking to him about his training and he mentioned that he had two standard runs. One was 9 miles, and because he ran in a hilly area (whereas the marathons he ran were flat) he estimated that the time he would take to run a full 26.22-mile marathon would be three times as long as it took him to run 9 miles. In other words, he more or less balanced the reduction in his 9-mile speed that would occur over the much longer distance with the fact that he ran 9 miles much more slowly on the hills than he would do on the flat.

His other standard run was half the distance—$4\frac{1}{2}$ miles. When estimating the time he would take to run a marathon, he used a $\times 6$ multiplier—in other words he applied the same multiplier as if he had run twice the distance, 9 miles. Quick as a flash, I pointed out the error of his ways—that he should use a $\times 6\frac{1}{2}$ or $\times 7$ multiplier to compensate for the fact that he was only running half the distance.

My neighbour in return quickly pointed out the error of my ways and the false assumption I had been making. What was that assumption? Well, his $4\frac{1}{2}$-mile run was considerably more hilly than his 9-mile run! So, when considering a problem or issue, we need to follow this simple process:

1. Identify: what are all the assumptions we could be making?

2. Check validity: why are we making them?

3. Remove invalid assumptions.

4. Discover better solutions.

I give some examples for you to do, known as lateral thinking questions, under the final section on group discovery, as you may want to do them with a work group or social group to prove that groups can think more creatively than individuals or, better phrased, individuals can become more creative as a result of being involved in an effective process of group discovery.

Techniques to improve creative thinking

Before looking at group discovery, we shall consider two other powerful techniques to improve creative thinking. The first of these techniques is provocation and the second is visualization.

Provocation

This technique was first discovered by Edward de Bono. In order to jerk the mind away from its comfortable path of logical thinking, you provoke it by deliberately reversing a key feature, contained in the problem, and provided that judgement is suspended and movement generated, sound ideas emerge from what appears to be an illogical statement. I shall provide two examples, one mentioned by de Bono, and the other the result of a 'head-bang how' session. After we had determined the 'whats' and 'whys' and started on the 'hows', a managing director of a firm of underwriting agencies (who did not give me permission to reveal his name) used this description, which I think is excellent. Normally, idea generation sessions are referred to as 'brainstorming'.

EXAMPLE

In the 1970s in the USA, an insurance executive was considering what new insurance product he could introduce into the life market to generate more sales and profits. A key feature was that the proceeds were paid after death. He used the provocation 'You die before you die', suspended judgement and generated movement. The successful product was a new policy, which paid out three-quarters of the death benefit to policy holders who became terminally ill before they died. This was a breakthrough in thinking and became an industry standard product.

Clearly, you cannot die before you die, and the use of logic (in the shape of criticism) would have destroyed the ability to create the new product. It seems very logical afterwards. No doubt his boss would have said:

> 'Well, clearly, if we know precisely when they are going to die, we can afford to pay out some of the proceeds before they actually do, perhaps charging a little early payment fee! The beneficiaries will be delighted to get their hands on the money sooner rather than later. The policy holder couldn't care less, or will be relieved that the costs of care will be covered or will like to see his beloved ones enjoying the money before he passes on—depending on the circumstances. A very logically sound proposition, which will improve our image and our profits. I am really rather surprised that I didn't think up the idea myself!'

Next, the 'head-bang how' example:

EXAMPLE   A group of managers were thinking up ways of improving creative thinking. One suggestion was to increase time spent thinking, as that would increase the number of ideas. The reverse suggestion was to spend no time at all!

Subsequent consideration of that led to recognition that some problems are best ignored as they go away (as they were not important after all) or get solved by someone else, and it is wise not to wrestle with a problem at night, but focus on getting to sleep, as you often wake up refreshed, having solved the problem in your sleep—the land of illogic and provocation.

Visualization

A picture is worth a thousand words. Dreaming or day-dreaming or wishful thinking along the lines of 'Wouldn't it be nice if ... ?', 'If only ... ', 'I wonder what would happen if ... ?' all help with ideas, but here we are considering deliberate or planned visualization.

Visualization is an excellent way of improving memory, as well as creativity. Let us assume that you have an appointment with the dentist before you go to work the following day. If, when you go to bed, you imagine putting a very large (exaggeration helps the memory) tube of toothpaste into the right shoe, which you place beside the bed, and dwell for a few moments on the image before you go to sleep. As soon as you awake, you will visualize the tube and remember the reason behind the image. Try it—it works. After all, pieces of paper can get lost.

Problem solving

As regards ideas, we shall demonstrate both the power of visualization and provocation to solve a problem.

A man is in the middle of an island surrounded by deep water. He is looking after a flock of sheep. (Don't worry how he and the sheep got there. You can assume omnipotent intervention or you are in a dream.) The island is covered by very tall grass, which is bone dry. A fire has started (omnipotent causation!) at the end of the island, furthest away from the sheep and the man. There is a wall of flame moving very slowly towards the man and his sheep. The wind is blowing directly towards the man, and will remain in the same direction throughout. How do the man and all the sheep remain alive and unburned, given that, if they enter the water, they will all drown?

A good starting open question is: 'What is available to the man to save his own and the sheep's lives?' It should be clear that the water is a no-go area. That leaves the sheep, the man with his strength and intelligence, the wind, the grass and the fire.

Sheep are large, awkward and stupid creatures. Avenues of thought like the man picking up a sheep and trying to put the fire out with it only lead to a man with a hernia and a severely burned sheep. So, let us assume that the sheep are passive bystanders, and turn to the wind.

Now the fact that the wind is moving in the same direction must have significance or it would not have been mentioned. This looks like a hindrance, but perhaps it is a help or even a clue to the answer. Let us get into our helicopters and visualize events over time. This will help our thinking. If we hover at a safe distance, we initially see a thin orange line, a little bit of black behind it, a substantial amount of green ahead slowly being eaten by the orange—and the little dots of the man and his sheep. As time passes, the black area expands and the green contracts. Eventually the orange line disappears, the dots no longer move—all is black. In our contemplative mood, we may notice that black is a sign of death—yet it is also a safety zone. If the man and his sheep were magically transported to a black zone, they would be safe. Fortunately, the man is a magician, as we shall see.

Now let us indulge deliberately in some reversal thinking, while still in the helicopter. The key feature is the constant direction of the wind, bringing death in its wake. Let us reverse it! What do we see? We see the line of fire falter, change direction briefly, before dying down and out. So let us become the man in this reversal scenario—reverse our perspective. From the man's perspective, he sees a wall of fire moving away from him briefly, before dying out and leaving a black area of safety. Now the man cannot reverse the direction of the wind, but can he create a situation where he sees fire moving away from him? If he can, he and his flock will be safe.

What about the speed of the wind? What are the implications of the fact that it is blowing very gently? They are: (1) the man has plenty of time to implement any stratagem, and (2) the man can outrun the wind.

What about the fire and the grass? How can they be used, with a man who can outrun the wind, to create the situation where the man sees fire moving away from him?

Have you got it now—has the answer come as a flash, as the result of the cumulation of questions, visualization and provocation? I bet it has.

The man produces a fire-break. He grabs some grass, twists it together, runs to the fire and lights the grass rope. He runs away from the fire, past the sheep to the other end of the island and starts his own fire—a fire moving away from him, reversing the direction of the wind! The original fire bears slowly down, and the new fire creeps to the end of the island, where it splutters and expires, leaving that now comforting and safe black zone. The man waits until the last moment, and herds his sheep to safety.

How to harness the power of group discovery

Let us now move from the individual level to the small group level and consider how to harness the power of group discovery. If you have a work group, you can very easily develop that group so that it produces synergy, i.e. it produces more creativity and better quality decisions than each individual acting independently.

This can be accomplished through 'questioning assumptions' questions—or lateral thinking questions, as they are more commonly known. However, to guarantee the result, you will have to sell the exercise on pages 65 and 66 to your team and follow the guidelines set out below.

As we know, we all make assumption that limit our ability to find good solutions. Each question contains an assumption or assumptions which, if uncovered, will lead to better solutions than would otherwise have been the case. There will be group discovery because different individuals will feed off different questions and comments to lead to new insights. Let us take an example.

EXERCISE   A woman jumps from the top of a New York skyscraper. It is a deliberate act of suicide. As she tumbles to her death, she hears a telephone ring. She cries out 'I wish I had not jumped'. Explain her behaviour.

Now the first point to make is that the exercise should generate laughter and fun (and humour is a great creative catalyst, as we know). So everyone should be encouraged to suggest answers, with no criticism of those answers. (You will need to explain the no criticism rule and reasons in advance.) Suppose someone says (if you were using this one by way of example) that she thought she was dying of cancer, and the doctor had promised to confirm the results an hour ago. She had waited and waited and then jumped. When she heard the telephone, she wished she had not, in case the news was good. Then be positive about this suggestion, check what assumption is being made to produce this answer and encourage different answers. Specifically, try to focus the group on considering what assumptions are being made. All the information is in fact relevant, and no information not provided is relevant.

As I have said, and you should confirm, there is no wrong answer, but better solutions are developed if someone picks on the 'indefinite article' in front of the word 'telephone'. It is 'a' telephone and not 'the' telephone. If people assume, as many do, that it is 'the' telephone, then they create stories in which the caller is known to the woman. If they realize that it is 'a' telephone, then they think up stories in which a complete stranger has made the call. Explanations might be a 'neutron' holocaust, where the woman was convinced she was the only person left alive, could not bear the isolation or the more prosaic deafness, and regretted her suicide decision when she heard a telephone ring.

A 'questioning assumptions' exercise is set out below. If group discovery works, which it almost invariably does, you can have a short review at the end to confirm some basic points.

If asked, 'Do you feel that, if you had worked on these problems on your own, you would have done so well or enjoyed yourselves as much?', the answer from all will be 'No'—confirming the reality of group discovery.

If asked, 'Did you find, on occasions, that the answer came as a flash to one individual, and not the same one, but that flash of insight or inspiration was helped by the comments and questions of other members of the group', all will say 'Yes', confirming how we can all be more creative than we think we are, and, again, the power of positive group interaction.

Finally, you may be asking 'Where are the answers?' For you and your team to derive maximum value, no one should know these in advance. And, for many, there is not 'one right answer'. In fact, the final rule you should tell your team is that if someone knows the answer, he or she should not blurt it out, as it will spoil the fun for the others. On the other hand, just being silent and excluded is not a good idea—so he or she can help the group by asking them questions that will enable them to find the false assumption or assumptions for themselves.

Some suggested answers are given at the end of Chapter 11 (page 142), but you should resist the temptation to look until you have completed the exercise with your team.

Questioning assumptions EXERCISE

1. A little girl is standing with her parents by a river, looks at their reflection in the water, and says: 'I can see all four of us.' How can this be, when there are only three people present?

2. A man goes out, sells his dog and is killed on the way home. How did he die?

3. A woman is found dead, hanging from the rafters 10 feet from the ground in a totally empty room. There is a pool of water beneath her. How did she die?

4. A man is pushing a car, which stops next to an hotel. The man immediately realizes he is bankrupt. Explain.

5. How do you plant four solid spheres so that the centre of each sphere is exactly the same distance from the centre of all the other spheres?

6. An archaeological team discover two very well-preserved bodies, while excavating. They positively identify the bodies as the original, biblical Adam and Eve. How can this be?

7. A naked man is found dead in the desert, clutching a straw. In his immediate vicinity, there is nothing but sand. Beyond the sand in one direction lies a number of hills. Think up an explanation that takes account of all the facts.

What are the strategies?

To end this chapter, we look at the key strategies to ensure that the discovery technique can become a way of life for a work group, the pitfalls to avoid and the benefits that will be enjoyed. I assume that, for whatever reason, you did not want to apply the questioning assumptions approach with a work group.

The key strategies are given below.

Explain and apply the golden rules

The rule of no criticism by word and body language needs to be understood and agreed by all beforehand and then monitored by the facilitator, whether you or someone else is appointed to the role.

If there is criticism, which may well occur initially, make sure there is no criticism of the individual who is criticizing(!)—assume it is unintended (which it may well be, especially if it is non-verbal), and gently point it out as unintended and carry on. For example:

'Joanna. I know you did not mean to—but there was negative body language when Simon suggested "less overtime". It is important that we keep any criticism until the evaluation stage. OK?'

So 'silly' ideas must be tolerated, as they would be killed off under the withering fire of criticism, and can lead to new insights and useful perspectives. Silliness for its own sake is not a good idea, but the de Bono techniques of reversal—reversing the logic of an idea or exaggerating it— can be very useful. Generating atmosphere with a few dry runs on some humorous issues is recommended. There can be an enormous difference in output between a group that is cold and hesitant and one that is relaxed and smiling.

A flipchart or whiteboard will be necessary so that there is a visual display of ideas or the group can stick 'Post-it' notes around the walls. In the former case, there will need to be a scribe or facilitator, who is also a contributor. In the latter case, the ideas should be verbally articulated as well as written down. In both cases, someone needs to ensure that the no criticism rule is followed.

Agree and implement a time plan

Agree a timetable. It does not have to be long, e.g. 15 minutes for initial set of ideas, 5 minutes prioritizing, 30 minutes for development and action planning. It may be necessary to be flexible: if ideas are still coming after 15 minutes, don't cut them off. But having a framework and a sense of urgency helps to develop focus and creativity. Usually, you will find that 15 minutes is more than ample.

Agree a scoring mechanism

There is no need to differentiate between action areas and alternative actions. Given that 'strategy means focus and hard choices', you can agree with the group a simple scoring mechanism where each member selects what he or she thinks are the most viable to develop and ranks the top 3, 4 or 5 (depending on number of ideas). A useful rule of thumb is to have 1 point for 6 ideas. So if there are 30, ask the individuals to pick their top 5, and if there are 15, to pick their top 3.

Also, by adopting this approach, criticism becomes implicit rather than explicit—so no egos are bruised. You will find that there are variations but often a consensus emerges around the top few—which is great for motivation and commitment—generating a shared vision of what needs to be done and why.

Finally apply the how/how approach to each action concept selected, or, if the idea is already in action format, determine and answer the other open questions like 'What kind of incentives?', 'What proportion of team regards?' 'What sort of training?', 'When?' and 'By whom?'.

What are the pitfalls?

There are a few pitfalls to avoid. Putting these, using reversal as positive actions, we have:

Use the right numbers

Many experts recommend up to 20 people present, acknowledging that some individuals will not contribute—presumably sacrificing atmosphere and the individual on the altar of quantity. The group discovery technique (GDT) is best as a team or small group process, with numbers not exceeding eight, nor less than four.

Focus on quality

There can be a temptation to go for quantity rather than quality. One writer and practitioner proudly told his readers that he had achieved, through one 'brainstorming', over 100 restatements of the problem and over 1000 ideas! Evaluation took months, and everyone lost interest!

Quality is much more important. Usually, you will get 20 or so initial ideas, which is excellent, especially as less than one-quarter are likely to make it to the action planning stage. The no criticism rule must take primacy, but it is worth creating an environment where there is no pressure for contribution and where silence is recognized as a creative act.

Avoid the special event syndrome

The GDT or 'brainstorming' can be seen as a major and rare event, reserved for a major strategic issue attended by a select group, usually off-site and expensive. There is a place for that, especially where the top team is involved, but it can give the wrong cultural messages—particularly that GDT is not a cheap, effective, work-based regular group activity.

Keep the same group throughout

Sometimes, GDT is carried out in isolation. Evaluation is done later, occasionally by different people. The GDT should be an integral part of problem solving and action planning, carried out by the same people and often in the same session, as it is part of a clearly defined process.

What are the benefits?

The creative output will be far higher than that of any individual, as the synergy exercise should have demonstrated. We all have our mindsets, our limited background, experience and knowledge. By opening our minds, sharing our ideas and allowing those sparks to be generated, we all become more creative and the whole always exceeds the sum of the individual parts.

This also holds for developing the initial set of ideas and evaluation. We can only tap into ourselves. The combined wealth of knowledge and experience of the group makes development and evaluation quicker and more effective.

Fundamental improvements in work processes will occur. The GDT can be applied to issue identification, problem solving, project definition, writing a scoping paper, planning and so on. In fact, whenever there is an open question to be asked, GDT should be applied. It can be used for group tasks and individual tasks at any vital stage. Increasingly, it becomes informal and swift. Other team members are happy to help the individual for four reasons:

1. It improves the efficiency and effectiveness of a colleague's output.

2. As it is reciprocated, it improves the efficiency and effectiveness of their own work.

3. The knowledge of the group about each individual's key work activities expands enormously. This makes it much easier to take up the reins when a colleague is sick or on leave.

4. Team morale soars.

It is the way to generate a shared vision, common understanding, agreed objectives and a sense of unity and direction—it is the pivotal team-building tool.

6

How to become more persuasive

The art of being a successful leader lies in getting people to do what you want them to do because they want to do it.
FRANKLIN D. ROOSEVELT

What this chapter covers

In this chapter, we look at persuasion, and consider how we can effectively persuade another person in the three general situations:

1. Where we want to persuade someone to do something we want, and the other party has no specific agenda, but has some authority like a boss (or parent), and we need to persuade him or her if we are going to succeed.

2. Where we want to persuade the other party to make some change—to do something differently from what they are currently doing.

3. Where each of us has a different agenda, our circumstances ensure interaction and there is thus the potential for conflict. There has to be an effective dialogue to resolve it—to negotiate an outcome that satisfies both parties.

In each case we establish the key strategies and exemplify them by case study or conversation, analysing the conversations from a questioning perspective.

How to persuade someone in authority to do something we want

We look first at the key strategies we need to adopt, and then at a real-life situation and conversation that illustrates key points.

Key strategies

There are eight key strategies.

Apply the PBA rule

PBA (Perceived Balance of Advantage) is a very simple and very powerful concept. If, during any stage of the discussion, the persuadee (the other party—in this case the person in authority) perceives that there is a balance of advantage to be gained in the proposition, then he or she will accept it.

This means that we, in the role of persuaders, should try to assume the role of the persuadee and, in advance of the persuasion meeting, identify what that person will perceive as a positive or negative aspect in our proposal. We need to know his or her value system, where he or she is coming from—what makes the persuadee tick. In the case of a boss, for instance, this is likely to be known as we shall already have formed a relationship.

The situation in which we have never met the persaduee (like the first meeting with a prospective client) is dealt with in the final chapter, 'How to delight your client'.

Don't be menu driven

We also have to consciously and deliberately avoid being menu driven. What happens, especially when it is a matter of considerable importance to us, is that we marshal all our arguments in advance, cover off all the angles and develop a menu of points to be made. All these arguments tend to follow our own logic and value system. We carry out the discussion as if we were persuading ourselves all over again! This leads to the next point.

Know when you have won

While questioning skills are not so vital in this situation, listening skills are at a premium. Sometimes we succeed when we are not prepared to accept success! This often happens when we are menu driven and not listening. I have seen it many, many times. Early in the discussion, the persuadee indicates agreement. The persuader does not seize the moment and close down to action planning, if relevant, or terminate the meeting after the appropriate pleasantries. Instead, the persuader carries on to the next item on the agenda, with the irresistible logic that has been so carefully determined in advance. A growing sense of irritation on the part of the persuadee, leading to a change in mood, or another issue being mentioned that turns the persuadee off, and all is lost—defeat snatched from the jaws of victory.

What can also happen is that there is agreement to part of the proposition, but again that is not concluded and taken out of the conversation. The same fate often awaits.

Don't beat about the bush

Time is valuable, particularly the time of those in authority (from their perception), and so be crisp and clear. Let the persuadee know early on (assuming the objective has not been advised in advance) what you want and why.

Be positive

The more we display a positive and enthusiastic approach, the greater the probability of success. If we show how much we believe, that will be noticed—and remember that words are only the smallest part of the whole that is face-to-face communication. Vocal tone, facial expression and body language will be more convincing than mere words.

Accentuate the positive

To the extent that you can control the meeting, which will be difficult as the persuadee will be asking most of the questions, start with the positives, mention but minimize the negatives and keep a few positives up your sleeve to be used if and when necessary.

Be prepared

It is important both for your self-confidence and to increase the chance of success that you spend the time it takes before the meeting to work out your strategy, particularly the PBA aspect.

Be flexible

If you keep an open mind, maintain focus on the persuadee and listen effectively, you will be sufficiently flexible to achieve two important outcomes:

1. *Change an initial mindset.* We may think we have worked out all the PBAs, but there may have been some event or events in the persuadee's recent past that have caused some alteration—reduced the significance of one aspect or introduced a new one. By being flexible, we can adjust our strategy.

2. *Change our objective.* Sometimes, we can latch onto the wavelength of

the other party to such an extent that possibilities can emerge that are better than our original objective. By being flexible, we can win more that we dreamed possible. The tale of Nazaruddin illustrates this point:

Nazaruddin had some valuable carpets to sell in the marketplace. He spent the day in skilful negotiations with prospective purchasers. At the end of the day, he met his friend for a few drinks. Nazaruddin's hands were empty and his pockets jangled with the weight of silver in them. He was flushed with excitement and feelings of satisfaction—even triumph. 'I have done it. This is the best day of my life. My objective was twenty pieces of silver and I made forty. O frabjous day! Callooh! Callay!' (Nazaruddin was well read and had been a manager in former life!)

His friend commented with melancholy mien: 'But Nazaruddin. Those carpets were the most beautiful and valuable I have ever seen. You should have got far, far more than forty pieces of silver. You should have got forty pieces of GOLD!' To which Nazaruddin replied, with a slight shake of his head: 'What is this gold?'

We are limited by our knowledge, which determines our horizons. If we are flexible and have open ears, we can change both.

To end this section, let us consider another real-life situation and conversation.

CASE STUDY

A few years ago a group of managers on a senior executive programme were carrying out persuasion role-plays, dealing with important work-related issues. The objective was to learn more about how to be persuasive and to increase the probability of successful outcomes, when they had to do it for real.

One persuader, John, wanted to persuade his boss, played by Gerald, to allow him to move up North to expand a business line, which research had shown would be welcomed by customers and would make a good profit for his company.

The first attempt was a disaster. The persuader was rather full of himself, very strong on the benefits to the customer and the company, which he assumed would be clinchers, and occasionally was verbally aggressive. This was despite the fact that he had briefed the persuadee as to the key drivers of his boss—developing his empire, building his reputation and personal prestige and avoiding any significant change.

The project, as presented, represented major change, reduced his boss's empire, and the key message that emerged was just how good a move it would be for the persuader! The person playing the role of the boss—the persuadee—played it well, and inevitably turned the project down

All five of us had a chat. (There were two other managers, acting as observers and commentators until it was their turn.) The PBA and the other approaches were discussed, John spent some time formulating his strategy and the role-play was re-run. It was successful. I was advised by John a few weeks later that he had also been successful with his real boss in the real world. Let us look at the conversation, encapsulating the new approach.

Gerald: Come in and sit down, John. I can give you no more than half-an-hour, as I have a meeting with Callum (the MD) at 11. What do you want?

John: Thanks very much for seeing me, Gerald. I want your permission for me to move to Edinburgh to open up the Scottish mobile phone market.

Gerald: Why on earth do you want to do that? You are doing very well down here, your existing business is expanding, and you form an important part of my team. I don't want to lose you.

John: You won't lose me Gerald. I think it is important that there is continuity, so I suggest that I report directly to you, as now, but also have a dotted line into Tim (the Northern Region manager).

Gerald: I see. That makes sense—but there is still going to be a lot of disruption. To begin with, I would need to find someone to take over your role.

John: Hardly any disruption at all, Gerald. I have already had a word with Personnel, and they have one or two internal candidates, who they think you would approve of. In any case, I would not move until the new person was in place, and I had handed over the reins. We mustn't rush into these things.

Gerald: Oh! I agree completely. But there is always a chance that the business will fail, and I don't want that to happen.

John: We have carried out detailed research—the market is ripe and will expand rapidly. We shall be first in and gain a competitive edge. We have succeeded down South against tough competition. We shall succeed even more up North with no competition, and we shall all benefit, politically speaking from being part of a success story.

Gerald: I see, I see. You may well have something in this new project. I am in favour, in principle.

John: That's great, Gerald. I'll give you all the research papers and business plan by the end of the week, and get onto Personnel straightaway, so that you can look at the CVs of suitable candidates to replace me. Thanks very much for your support.

Analysis

John had to make a fundamental shift in attitude and approach to be successful. He was very much a 'can-do' person, keen to make things happen quickly. However, once he starting viewing the proposition from his boss's perspective—put his PBA hat on—he realized that he had to be conservative, and plan accordingly. What is more, he was proactive, both in developing strategies to accommodate his boss's conservatism, and cater for his key drivers *before* the actual meeting. Specifically:

- Allowing his boss to remain his boss (knowing full well that out of sight would be out of mind) so that the boss's empire would expand.
- Liaising with Personnel to ensure that the replacement issue was covered.

- Confirming that the new person would be in place before leaving.
- Focusing the benefits on enhancing his boss's credibility and personal reputation, but in a subtle 'we' approach.
- Taking responsibility for all subsequent actions, to minimize the impact of the change on his boss.

Another very effective approach was the use of language, that mirrored his boss's own conservative orientation. (We shall examine this in more detail in the final chapter on client relationships.) Specifically:

- 'I think it is important there is continuity.'
- 'Hardly any disruption at all.'
- 'We mustn't rush into these things' (which received enthusiastic agreement from Gerald!).
- 'We have carried out detailed research.'

As mentioned earlier, this situation is not one where you, as the person doing the persuading, are full of open questions (John asked no questions at all), but where you have thought through all the angles from the other person's perspective before you meet, implemented any necessary actions before the meeting (e.g. liaising with Personnel), ensured that you talk the same language as the persuadee during the meeting, and listen effectively throughout.

We now turn to the next persuasion situation.

How to persuade someone else to do something differently

There are three basic choices, and three basic types of relationship to consider (see Table 6.1). We look at the three generic strategies in turn.

Promote discovery

The heart of this book has been how to use the right open questions in the right way in the right order to promote discovery (by both parties) and thereby create an effective relationship that leads to positive action—building the confidence and competence of both parties. What we haven't covered is just why this is so powerful and effective from a psychological perspective (see Figure 6.1).

To make the point, we first take the extreme, but increasingly prevalent, situation in today's business world of when we are suddenly told to do something we don't want to do. It could vary from being told we have lost our jobs (as faced Jenny and Harry in Chapter 4) to being told to change

Table 6.1   Strategies to persuade others to change

	Generic approach		
Nature of relationship	Tell	Sell (using PBA)	Promote discovery
Upwards	No	Only if asked (what and why; involve in how)	Yes
Across	No	Only if asked (what and why; involve in how)	Yes
Downwards	When insecure (what, why and how)	Only if asked (what and why; involve in how)	Yes

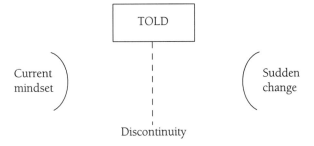

Shock, disbelief, rejection, resistance, awareness, anger, blame –
loss of self-esteem

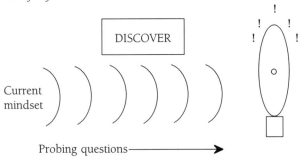

Figure 6.1   *The power of discovery.*

our behaviour (being criticized in an area in which we believed we were competent). The change is necessarily unconnected with our current view of the world, and represents a very unpleasant new world. All of us will react along the lines indicated, which describe the first part of the reaction or transition curve. In time order, there is shock, disbelief, rejection, resistance, awareness, anger, blame and eventually acceptance and regret. During this phase our self-esteem takes a heavy blow—our competence and confidence reduces.

There are different impacts and degrees of pain, depending on the degree of trauma the change represents, how confident we are at the beginning and whether we are an extrovert or introvert. I would recommend those who are interested in exploring change management in depth to read my earlier book: *Creating Growth from Change: how you react, develop and grow* (McGraw-Hill, 1994).

We do not like being told what to do, especially if it is unexpected, so in most circumstances (we shall look at the exception when we consider the 'tell' strategy after the 'sell' strategy) telling someone else to do something different will be ineffective. They will resist and their competence to do it will be reduced.

The problem is compounded, when we are the boss and have positional power. Because of that power, our direct report will verbally agree to doing what we ask. However, we shall find, later, that either there are endless delays in the execution of the promise or it is carried out badly. This makes us think the subordinate is incompetent or stroppy and fail to recognize that that is merely an effect (unrelated to the actual competence or personality of the subordinate) and the cause was, in fact, our own incompetence! (We shall discuss these perception gaps in detail in Chapter 10.)

Let us refer again to Figure 6.1. Providing we have the patience, have planned and have well-developed questioning and listening skills, we promote discovery of the change we want the other party to make. What happens, putting ourselves in the shoes of the person being persuaded, is that we start from our original position or mindset, and, as our thinking is probed, it slowly shifts and then the new idea, concept, action hits us in a flash. You may well have experienced this, when and if you carried out the 'Questioning assumptions' exercise on pages 67 and 68 with a work or social group.

The key point is that because we have discovered the 'what' and 'why' ourselves, we shall understand the change and be committed to make it happen. We shall be fully 'empowered'—because we have empowered ourselves. Incidentally, effective empowerment only occurs where the decision-making area of the individual is enlarged, and the quality of the decisions taken are improved, which can only occur if there has been a process of discovery.

However, in order to implement the change effectively, we shall need support. So we *promote discovery* in the other party and then *provide support.*

Let us now look at a complete example of promoting discovery and providing support.

Example

We have already covered the case of effectively promoting discovery. At the start of this book, we had the 'tell' case, where the managing director told his senior manager, Tim, to transfer Charles from delivery to sales. Tim, in turn, simply summoned Charles into his office and told him. Let us recall Charles's reaction:

> Charles walked slowly towards the toilets—he couldn't face his colleagues in the open plan office. He shook his head slightly in stunned surprise and temporary disbelief. He locked himself in the toilet and sat for a while on the seat, saying nothing but with a slight glistening in his eyes. Then, if you could have been there, you would have caught a few words, spoken softly but with passionate intensity. 'The bastards! The bloody bastards.'

This is a powerful demonstration of an individual going through the reaction curve!

Now, we shall recall the conversation that John (the effective senior manager) had with Charles (promoting discovery of the change), analyse the questions deployed, and then move on to the continuation of the conversation, demonstrating how effective support was provided to ensure that Charles left fully confident and competent to implement the change. Remember that John had been assertive with his boss, the managing director, and got a three-month transition period. Additionally, he had planned the strategy and the meeting, so that the change would be introduced as part of a regular review process.

Conversation

'So, Charles, let's consider how your role should best develop in the next year or so. As a starting point, let us look at what you do well. What are your views?'

'Well, er,' Charles commenced after a short pause to gather his thoughts; 'delivering the service to the client. The exact nature of the service and timing of delivery is agreed in the proposal I get. I know our services backwards, my communication skills are good and I satisfy the client according to the agreed contract. What's more, I enjoy it, and the clients know I do, and that makes the service I provide even better.'

'Agreed', said John. 'There is no doubt that you perform very well in meeting the client's service needs. But what about selling? You do well there too.'

'Well I don't do much selling. And what I do is not proper selling', came Charles's reply.

'What do you mean precisely?' John asked.

'Well the business I get is nearly all from existing clients, where I have already proved my competence, and who appreciate our company. So it is easy to sell more of the same service or sell different services that my colleagues actually deliver. I do not, like the full-time sales staff, follow up leads that come in via the telephone sales teams. That's not my role, and, what's more, I'm not an aggressive, pushy type.'

'No you certainly are not', agreed John. 'Let me ask you. Why do our customers buy our services?'

Charles paused before replying: 'Because they believe that our service will meet their needs, and will provide value for money spent.'

'And who creates that belief?' was the next question from John.

'Well the salesperson, of course', came the instant reply from Charles.

'And how does the salesperson create that belief, without which there will be no purchase decision?' John continued probing.

'He builds the relationship and creates trust in himself as well as the service.' Charles was getting absorbed in the discussion.

'Yes, a good salesperson sells himself. Most service decisions or employment decisions for that matter are made as a direct result of the quality of the relationship the salesperson or the prospective employee creates with the purchaser. People buy people not products. You have excellent skills in communication and developing relationships. So, Charles, are you a good salesperson?'

'Well, put like that, the answer must be yes', came Charles's reply. 'I hadn't really thought about it before in those terms. But, yes, you are right. I am a good salesperson, but I prefer delivering the service.'

'Naturally so,' said John, 'as you are good at that, comfortable with it and spend most of your time working in that area. But there is something else to consider. In your opinion, how many competent service deliverers do we have?'

'Well,' mused Charles, 'I think the whole team is competent, one reason why we are getting so much repeat business.'

'I agree. What about good salespersons, taking the definition we have agreed?' asked John.

'Well, quite a few aren't up to scratch. Organizationally, we are better at delivery than selling', replied Charles.

'Again, I agree', said John. 'So, from an organizational perspective, which is the priority—finding a good salesperson or a good deliverer?'

'Well, obviously, a good salesperson.' Charles was following the logic quickly now, and was sitting back in his chair in a very relaxed position. Then he paused for a moment or two, leaned forward and with some animation said: 'Just a minute, I begin to see where all this is leading. You want me to do more selling, don't you?'

'Got it in one, Charles,' John smiled, 'and not just me, but our beloved MD as well.'

Analysis

Let us examine these questions to confirm their nature and how discovery was produced:

- 'What are your views?'—'involving' what.

- 'What about selling?'—'identifying' what, introducing a key issue.

- 'What do you mean precisely?'—'probing thinking' what.

- 'Why do our customers buy our services?'—'asking for an explanation uncritically' why.

- 'Who creates that belief?' While John knows the answer, he deliberately goes the 'open' route to promote discovery.

- 'How does the salesperson create that belief?' 'Probing thinking' how (used after 'what' and focusing Charles's thinking to lead to the desired conclusion).

- 'Are you a good salesperson?' The only closed question, getting specific agreement of the first planned discovery, which has been achieved—Charles has changed his initial mindset that he was not a good salesperson to that, actually, he is. This is a necessary initial step to promoting discovery that he should switch to sales. If we believe we are good at something, we are much more likely to switch to that full time and be effective, than if we believe we are bad at it!

- 'How many competent service deliverers do we have?'—'establishing facts' how, and starting the process of discovery of the need for the switch.

- 'What about good salespersons, given the definition we have agreed?'—'probing for facts' what.

- 'Which is the priority—finding a good salesperson or a good deliverer?' The final nail in the discovery coffin, leading to the light bulb!

However, as stated earlier in this chapter, it is not sufficient just to promote discovery, but also to provide support—to ensure that the legitimate concerns and worries any significant change produces are raised and dealt with. Let us continue the conversation:

Providing support

'Oh! dear,' Charles said instinctively, 'that puts a different complexion on things. I had not realized until just now that this was not an academic discussion. You had a hidden agenda, after all, John.'

'I had and have three objectives—to get you to realize that you are excellent at managing relationships and therefore a good salesperson, to get you to appreciate that there is an organizational need for a good salesperson and to persuade you to switch your role from service delivery to selling', came John's reply.

'Well, John, you have succeeded on the first two, but I'm not very comfortable with the switch despite appreciating the logic of it', Charles said a little nervously. He liked and respected his boss, but had picked up the clear, though implicit, message that he didn't have much choice with the combined might of his boss and the MD behind the proposal.

'I can completely understand that. Any change, even if we logically recognize the need, will produce some negative emotions, as we are bound to feel worried about the unknown and concerned at leaving a known and comfortable past. Let us consider all your concerns and see if we can resolve them together.' John said this earnestly, looking directly and sympathetically at Charles.

Charles warmed to this reply. 'His boss did understand and cared', he thought. That helped ease a little of the tension that had crept over him. He didn't speak for a while, neither did John—but the silence was not oppressive.

'Well', Charles eventually broke the pause. 'As I said, I have no experience of following up the leads that come through the tele-sales team. I don't feel at all happy at having to do that.'

'No problem, Charles. No problem at all. I have checked with Personnel, and there is an excellent three-day residential programme run by the Salter centre on Sales Skills Development. We have sent a number of our sales staff on that, and they have returned with glowing reports, and what's more important, new found confidence and competence in following warm leads to a successful conclusion. As you appreciate, there is no cold-calling—simply following leads from the tele-sales girls or meeting actual or prospective clients, who come to see us or we go to see, as a result of leveraging the networks established or quality service provided by your colleagues.'

'That's excellent.' Charles showed a more positive response for the first time. Without knowing it consciously, he was beginning to get used to the idea, and accept it. 'So when would I go on this programme, before or after I switch into sales? Come to think of it, when do you suggest I make the switch?'

'Well, I think it is very important that you feel positive about the change, before it actually takes place. So I think that the switch should be gradual and not be completed for three months. The priority is to get you onto the Sales Skills Development programme as soon as possible. Fortunately, they run once a month—so could you liaise with Pauline in Personnel straightaway. She'll give you all the details and do all the administration for you.'

'OK', replied Charles. 'But what if I have a clash with a client on the service delivery side?'

'Good point', came John's reply. 'If there is a clash, you will need to explain that reality to the client as soon as possible, and the reasons for it, and have a substitute with whom the client is familiar and comfortable lined up in advance. That should solve that problem, but if you run into any difficulties, let me know and I'll help sort it out. Is that OK?'

'Yes, that's fine', replied Charles. The conversation tailed off again, but not for long.

'Charles, what other concerns or questions do you have about the move into sales?', John asked.

'Well,' said Charles, after reflecting for a moment, 'will I get more money?'

'The short-term answer is no, but the longer term answer is probably yes', said John.

Charles looked quizzically at his boss, who continued. 'As you know, there is a freeze on recruitment, which is why we have asked you to switch roles, and there is currently a freeze on pay increases and promotions. Both of us have to accept those constraints. So nothing this year. However, next year may be different, as we are beginning to enjoy some steady growth in business—it looks as if we have turned the corner. In the longer term, by combining excellence in service delivery with excellence in selling, you significantly increase your value to the organization and therefore significantly increase the possibility of promotion and the probability of enhanced financial reward.'

'Well that's fair enough', Charles responded.

'What else can I help you with?' came John's final question.

'Nothing at the moment, thanks John', replied Charles.

'Well, if you do think of anything, you know that you just need to ask and I'll do my level best to help.'

'I appreciate that', and Charles meant it.

'Well, don't forget to talk to Pauline about the programme and check on any clash with clients. Good luck, and thanks for responding so positively to the change.' With that, the two shook hands and Charles left.

Points to remember

Before we move on to the next generic strategy, 'sell', remember these three points:

1. Tease out the concerns using open questions.

2. Give direct, factual answers to the concerns raised.

3. Anticipate these concerns in advance by *thinking through the consequences of the change from the perspective of the person affected*, and have determined effective answers in advance.

Sell (using PBA)

In Chapter 3, one of the suggested 'dos' was to 'Provide answers, when asked'.

Recalling from that section:

> There can be a danger that we get into an exclusive open question mindset, and always end answering a question with a question! Sharing your experience and giving your opinion is a vital part of a leadership role and of any effective conversation. Often people lack confidence and need guidance and support. The trick is to try to build up confidence, promote discovery and develop thinking. Place the problem monkey back on the shoulders where it should rightly rest—by asking all the right open questions. However, if and when you are asked for your opinion or your experience, then freely give it. The point is not to impose it early on, but to pull first and push later (if asked). Too often, we simply push with all those closed, leading, logical alternative questions—and there is no real dialogue.

So, our core strategy should be to promote discovery, but if we are asked 'What exactly do you want me to do?' then we need to give the answer. However, we should have thought through the PBA aspects in advance, so that we sell the 'what' and the 'why' from their perceptions and not our own.

Finally, as with promoting discovery, we should try to hold an effective dialogue on the 'how' and provide effective support—have answers up our sleeve to all the concerns the change will create.

Now to the final strategy—'tell'.

Tell

Telling bosses what to do is not recommended! Telling peers what to do will not develop the relationship—nor will they do it! However, if we are the leader there are occasions when we *should* tell a subordinate what to do. Specifically, if there is a crisis, then it is our role to resolve it. Imagine the Captain of the *Titanic*, when the iceberg had struck, calling all his officers together and saying:

> 'Gentlemen, we have a problem. We have just been struck by an iceberg. So let us pour ourselves a stiff drink, eh, and have a chin-wag—a brainstorm to promote discovery of the various options, and then some time for action planning, with, of course, a full review of the plan, before implementing it. It's 3 p.m., and if we get started now, we should be ready for effective action in 4 hours!'

Of course not. As leaders, we seize control and tell our followers what to do, and why and how to do it so that the crisis is rapidly resolved.

I would emphasize that we do not simply tell people what to do, as some leaders do; we must also give a clear explanation of the crisis or reason requiring the action we suggest. Nor is covering 'what' and 'why' sufficient, we must give clear guidance on the specifics of the 'how'.

> 'Gentlemen, we have been hit by an iceberg. We must abandon ship immediately with a minimum of panic. Harry, you will be responsible for managing the news to the passengers and organizing their move to the life-boats; Sandy, you will be responsible for getting the passengers onto the life-boats and lowering them to the sea, applying the principle of women and children first; Charles, you will send out distress signals. Robert will … [and so on]. The sequence I propose is …
>   'Any questions, gentlemen? No? Then proceed to action.'

Where a specific follower is new to a job, and likely to lack confidence and be feeling insecure, then we need to 'tell' in a constructive way—provide clear guidance on what needs to be done, why and how.

We now move to the final section of this chapter, which pulls together a lot of the issues we have considered separately.

How to deal with potential conflict

Here, we are dealing with the position where each party has an agenda, the situation causes interaction, and so there is the potential for conflict. The possible outcomes are summarized in Figure 6.2. When considering each outcome, we shall refer back to earlier scenarios as well as a new scenario, based on a true story. The situation was a widower with a young daughter, who was a budding but bad pianist, and practised at the piano each evening during the week for a few hours.

They lived in a tenement block where a party wall separated them from a single woman—a lover of classical music—who regularly played her stereo. The party wall was thin so that the girl's endless practice each evening severely disrupted the women's ability to listen to the music, and the playing of the hi-fi severely disrupted the girl's ability to practise in peace!

We shall look at each problem in turn.

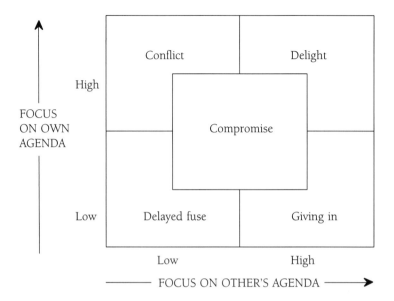

Figure 6.2   *Possible outcomes.*

Delayed fuse

This is where both parties avoid the conflict—both lose, as neither is satisfied. However, inevitably the blood of one or other party will boil over, and there will be some sort of confrontation, the outcome to which will vary.

Giving in

There can be aggression by one party and submission by the other, which would appear to lead to a clear winner, the aggressor, and a clear loser, the one who gives in. In the short term that is true, but not the long term.

If we take the switch into sales, enforced on Charles by Tim, the bad senior manager, then Tim won (got his way by abusing positional power) and Charles lost. In the longer term, both could be losers. Charles leaves as soon as he can switch back to his comfortable delivery, which won't look good for Tim in the eyes of the MD, or Charles stays but is not very competent, which means that the company has lost a good employee and gained a bad one, and Tim appears badly in the eyes of his boss—not running a good ship.

Again, in that cameo where the subordinate was brutally told off for his lateness, his boss won in the short term, but leaves the problem unsolved and a demotivated employee—not a winning outcome.

Conflict

If both parties are aggressive (focusing exclusively on their perceived rights), then conflict is inevitable. In the musical scenario, conflict of a non-physical nature occurred one evening when the little girl, fed up with the noise of the hi-fi, began to hit the piano louder and louder. The single woman responded by turning up the hi-fi louder and louder. This continued for some time until an unexpected resolution occurred—there were knocks on both doors, which, when opened, revealed the police, summoned by the neighbours!

When a conflict situation is materializing or has materialized, there are three possible outcomes over and above both parties losing. The first is: one wins and the other loses. We have already encountered this situation with Jenny, the lawyer. Remember this works only if the relationship is ceasing, and was achieved by using the 'assertive pause' to avoid tumbling down the reaction curve, powerful probing questions, righteous anger (not aggression) and clear logic. This form of assertive aggression produced a lose situation for George, her immediate boss (who walked out of his own office), and for the Personnel partner, Peter, who handed over £20 000!

However this type of situation tends to be exceptional and the first of the other two general outcomes is compromise.

Compromise

In the musical scenario, the advent of the police triggered a discussion between the adults, which led to a rota system: (1) the daughter practised on four nights a week and the woman wore headphones, and (2) the daughter did not practise on three nights a week and the woman played her music without headphones.

This is often the outcome of a standard negotiating position where each party gives up a little in order to gain a little. If we take the example of purchasing a car, then each party will have a range of acceptable prices. For instance, the seller may be prepared to sell for between £3500 and £4000 and the purchaser will buy between £3250 and £3750. Compromise is possible if there is an overlapping range, which in this case is £3500–£3750. There are now two fundamental strategies to maximize value gained by both parties.

Apply the PBA rule

Work out what aspects or features are perceived as maximizing value to the other party. For instance, let us assume you are the seller of the car, and have a nice stereo system, which you intend to leave, as you are buying a car with a more modern CD ROM system. You pick up, through your excellent questioning and listening skills, that the buyer is an enthusiastic music lover and really wants the stereo system to remain. You can negotiate away what is unimportant to you, but is very important to the other party, thereby increasing the price you get and increasing the perceived value given.

Maximize the perception of value given

This is a related point. If you have obtained an acceptable deal, then deliberately maximize the perceived value the other party has gained. If the other party thinks he or she has won overall and has made a good deal, encourage that thinking. That maximizes the probability that nothing goes sour in the actual implementation or when rust is found in places where it was not expected!

Too often, negotiations are too competitive, and even when a deal is struck one party sticks in the psychological boot: 'Now we have done the deal, did you know I was quite prepared to sell for £300 less?' A very stupid approach indeed.

However, the optimal outcome is 'delight'.

Delight

Achieving delight should be the aim of all potential conflict situations. This is the genuine win/win outcome, where both parties are delighted by the outcome, and can only be achieved through the parties having an effective dialogue resulting in discovery of possibilities that were not there at the outset. How to promote discovery has been the heart of this book.

We already have had an example of a potential conflict situation, which led to delight in the long term. That was when the CEO (Cedric) summoned Harry into his office to sack him! Harry managed to relieve the situation by avoiding aggressive questioning. Key strategies to achieve delight in time order are:

- The assertive pause, to stop rushing down the reaction curve.
- Recognition of the other party's situation and explicitly acknowledging that person's rights—developing an understanding of and perceived empathy with the other party.
- Acknowledging the drawbacks to one's own position, on the basis of fact.
- A proactive assertion of the merits of one's case, based on facts.
- Positive suggestions from an empathetic base to enable a dialogue that produces discovery.

By adopting this approach, we guarantee a win/win, as will be evident as we conclude this chapter by looking at the attitude over time of the other party—moving from the 'aggressive' I to the 'discovery' we.

Phase 1

'Here is someone who is infringing my rights, doesn't understand my position, whom I don't like very much and has to be dealt with.'

Phase 2

'Good heavens, he does understand my position, and my problems and what's more he's sympathetic to them—not such a bad person after all.'

Phase 3

'Oh! dear—I had not appreciated that he didn't mean to do that or that I was actually in error myself.'

Phase 4

'We really must see a way round our problem. That's an interesting suggestion—let's discuss that and see what we can do to solve the problem.'

Phase 5

'That's really great—we can both have our cake and eat it, because the cake has got much, much bigger!'

How to run an effective meeting

What this chapter covers

Our lives are full of meetings both at work and in social and family settings, but do we leave these meeting with hearts aglow and a renewed sense of purpose? In fact, many managers and staff have to work as early birds or night owls on their own to complete all the tasks that were left as unfinished business at the many ad hoc or planned meetings they attended during the day.

This chapter starts with two short case studies of meetings in the workplace that did not work, then looks at why, generally, meetings go wrong. We then consider 'how to run an effective meeting', based on the experience of a manager, Hannah, in the workplace, and conclude with a summary of the questions that are asked and how to answer them to guarantee success.

Two case studies

The caring executive

A departmental head operating in a multinational company was responsible for around 100 staff, and was a great believer in the need for and power of effective communication. So he used to call monthly departmental meetings, provide the assembled staff with information about key corporate activity and the impact on the department and then ask for questions. He found that the few questions that were asked tended to come from the same people (the senior managers) and no question was very provocative, which he genuinely wanted.

So I asked him what his objective was? He replied that it was to brief his department on all the important issues and have a healthy debate about them—so that he could explain all the thinking behind them, he had not formally covered, and assuage any uncertainties his staff might have about the changes.

So I asked him another question: 'Assuming you were a junior member of staff, what sort of question would you ask in front of the entire departmental workforce, including your boss, his boss, and her boss, with the speaker, to whom the question was going to be posed, being your boss's boss's boss's boss?'

Enlightenment dawned. He only called short monthly meetings after that, the purpose of which was to provide critical information and act as a leader's 'pep talk'. The section heads were encouraged to hold regular team briefings with much smaller groups of staff, where debate was to be encouraged, and short reports of the questions and answers to be sent to him to enable him to cover any outstanding concerns in his departmental meetings.

The uncaring executive

There was a CEO of a small organization in which a staff attitude survey had been held. One particular general complaint was the very poor communications that existed. The CEO decided to improve the position by holding weekly briefing meetings with a question and answer session. The CEO found that, as the company was going through turbulent change, even secretaries asked awkward questions. He didn't like that, so he suggested that questions should be put in writing in advance. They duly were, but still these awkward questions came through.

Finally, his patience snapped and he advised all staff that while they could continue to put questions in advance, the actual meeting would be a top-down briefing only, and no questions would be permitted. Attendance dropped from around 75 per cent to start with to around 15 per cent.

His initial objective had been to have some real dialogue, which was desperately needed and highlighted in the staff attitude survey. When his actions demonstrated that the objective was simply a 'tell session', staff gave up.

Why meetings fail

If you ask groups of staff what annoys them or demotivates them about meetings in the workplace, you will get a common set of themes emerging, irrelevant of company, level, or industry. I provide below the comments from one group of employees.

- No agenda
- Too much control by the chairperson/leader
- A lack of commitment by other members
- Too much talking and not enough listening
- Too much attention to procedure and detail
- Individuals creating their own power base and splitting the meeting
- A weak chairperson/leader—too many red herrings and not enough control

- Having cold water poured on your ideas by the chairperson or other members
- Hidden agendas, and behind the scenes manoeuvres
- Poor time-keeping
- Not knowing what you have to contribute or what your role is
- Feeling excluded and isolated
- Too many people present
- No sense of direction or purpose
- Afraid to contribute for fear of being allocated extra work
- All a bit too cosy, with lots of social chit-chat, but no focus on the task.

If, by using the power of reversal thinking, we as the chairperson can so organize ourselves and the meeting to allow us to reverse all these negative factors, then we shall run effective meetings—and that is exactly what Hannah did.

How to hold an effective meeting

This process was developed and implemented successfully in the workplace by a manager, Hannah, working for a large service sector company. She was a delegate on an open programme I ran a few years ago, and told me her story, giving me permission to use it.

Hannah's successful system

CASE STUDY

The background was the follow-up to a company-wide staff attitude survey, devised and administered by external consultants. The survey, in the form of a detailed questionnaire, covered a wide range of issues, looking both internally and externally. The response rate was 50 per cent, and the initial follow-up was a glossy brochure to outline the main findings.

The next phase was a company-wide exercise where groups were to meet, discuss the key findings and implement agreed changes.

Generally, the follow-up process was a disaster—because the leaders of the groups were the bosses. They were supposed to 'empower' their groups, but had no training as facilitators—so adopted their normal leadership style. What is worse was that the internal problems identified from the survey were poor communication flows, low motivation, poor delegation, lack of strategic direction and so on—all the responsibility of the leaders running the meetings!

If those attending had been honest, they would be directly criticizing the bosses, asking them to discuss them! Political reality and cultural norms—the very norms the survey uncovered and the organization genuinely wanted to change—took over. No right-minded junior dared to raise criticisms in front of his or her boss, who was responsible for staff appraisal and promotion prospects!

Another problem was that the numbers attending each meeting were between 10 and 12—to save time. If you want everyone present to contribute to the discussions, numbers should not exceed 8.

However, Hannah's departmental head was an enlightened man, and when Hannah, with the recommendation of the Personnel department behind her, asked him if she could mastermind the feedback process, he readily agreed and supported her.

She ran 11 peer-group meetings of between 4 and 8 people (ensuring the right numbers), i.e. secretaries, clerks, officers, junior managers, middle managers, and one for the section heads (including her boss) and the head of department. The individual feedback from every meeting was that it was a success. Real issues had been raised and discussed, and effective solutions had been put forward. Invariably a positive, problem-solving atmosphere had been generated. Each individual left the meeting in the knowledge that his or her voice had been heard, and his or her ideas listened to. Ideas had been shared, common attitudes exposed and consensus solutions developed.

How was this achieved, especially as Hannah's approach was identical at every meeting and successful at every meeting? Remember we are talking about a range of staff from secretary to executive head.

The way she approached the challenge is set out in Figure 7.1. There were six main factors: prior involvement, preparation, vision, clarity of role, ground rules, and consistent control. We shall consider each in turn.

Prior involvement

Hannah's first step was to ignore the findings of the survey! Her customers were the departmental staff, and she wanted the agenda to be customer-driven. They had replied passively to the pre-set questions. Additionally, the only differentiation made in the survey had been between managers and non-managers.

So, under the signature of the head of department, she sent out a positive up-beat letter, asking each member of staff to complete and return a non-attributable questionnaire. The questionnaire was simplicity itself. They were to write down the four most important work-related or 'local' problems they faced and any suggested solutions, and the four most important external or 'global' problems the company faced and suggested solutions.

[In hindsight, Hannah realized that she should have achieved a balanced approach by asking for successes and the reasons for them, However, the survey focused on problems and set the tone, which Hannah did not question at the time. Accentuating the positive as well as the negative is a more effective approach to staff-related issues, which is one reason why the force field analysis technique, outlined in Chapter 5, is so powerful.]

The final detail was for the respondent to enter a letter code in a box to identify his or her role/position. Hannah had decided to run cross-section peer group meetings on the basis that there would be a commonality of problem and they would be more likely to open up if their boss was not present.

Finally, Hannah took the decision to suppress a video she was supposed to

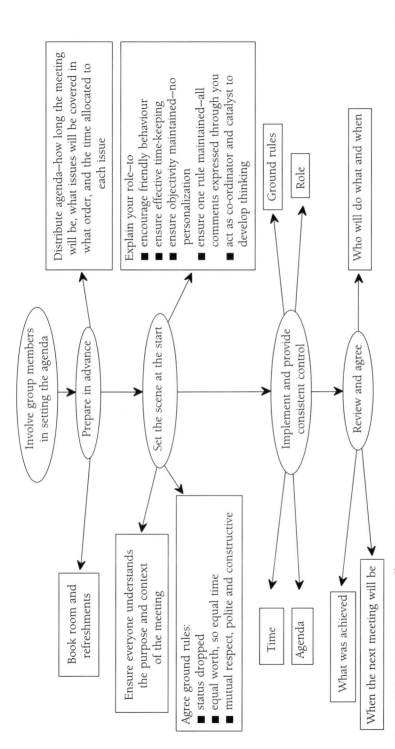

Figure 7.1 *How to run an effective meeting.*

show at each meeting, according to the facilitators' pack she had received. It was a bit of a disaster, she told me: 'The skills displayed by the "facilitating" boss were low, the level of interaction and the quality of debate was low, and the issues raised or actually discussed varied from the mundane to the trivial— one that took up a significant part of the video time was the quality of toilet paper in the ladies' loo!'

As mentioned, if the culture denies discussion of the important, and a discussion has to take place, then only the unimportant will surface.

Preparation

Hannah organized a meeting room of the right size and equipment, near but not part of the department, ensured that creature comforts were catered for, and the agenda—with the issues prioritized and the length of the meeting—was sent out well in advance. Little things, but if the basics are not attended to, it can be difficult to have lift off.

Vision

Hannah did not do much visioning, as the context was clear—the what and the why had already been established—but she did preface every meeting with a few comments about how rare it was for members of staff to be involved in solving real work-related issues, how important it was for them to take full advantage, and how she hoped they would show enthusiasm and commitment.

Clarity of role

Hannah made it crystal clear what her role was and why. This helped to manage expectations and generate certainty. For this particular exercise she was a facilitator, and explained that that meant that she would:

- encourage a friendly atmosphere;
- ensure that objectivity was maintained, e.g. there was no degeneration into personalities/grievances or identifying individuals, and any 'personal' problem could be expressed in general terms;
- ensure effective time-keeping;
- ensure that one rule was maintained throughout the meeting, i.e. all comments should be expressed through the facilitator as this would avoid meetings within meetings or comments becoming too personal;
- have no opinions herself (appropriate for a facilitator);
- act as a catalyst to develop thinking where blind alleys or cul-de-sacs occurred.

Ground rules

In describing her role explicitly, Hannah set some ground rules. Additional ones she set out were:

- Status should be dropped.
- At this meeting, everyone had equal worth and so she would try to ensure they had equal time to express their views.
- She hoped that individuals would show mutual respect and any comments on other people's views would be polite and constructive.

At the end of the introduction, she asked for comments and agreement to the approach, structure and rules. At no meeting was their any comment and everyone agreed verbally.

This was key. While most present, no doubt, genuinely agreed, one or two may well have been unhappy with certain aspects. However, it would not have looked good to have expressed their feelings, so they kept quiet and thereby gave Hannah the power she needed to ensure that what happened subsequently accorded with what she wanted to happen.

Consistent control

Having been given the power to proceed according to the rules, all Hannah had to do was ensure that they were kept.

- 'That's very interesting, John, but we have not heard from Julie yet, and, as you know, we are making sure that everyone has the opportunity to express a view. Julie, what do you think about formal meetings at peer group level between the sections?'
- 'Charles, please remember to address your comments through me.'
- 'Victoria. That comment is a bit personal. Remember, please, to talk in general terms, as we agreed. What you are saying—and correct me if I am wrong—is that the junior manager in your section does not hold any team meetings of clerical staff to improve the communication flow. Does anyone else have the same problem?'

Hannah had unwittingly replaced the negative power of the implicit by the positive power of the explicit and changed behaviour as a result.

It was certainly a novel approach to running a meeting, but Hannah told me that she had to try what was a culturally radical approach, because of the dimensions of the problems she knew she faced.

Most members of staff were sceptical and some were cynical. Being a large company, with years of success until the winds of change blew into a gale, it was still locked into a culture where behaviours accorded to established norms, based on hierarchy, status, conformity and the individual. Such environments are the breeding ground for scepticism and cynicism! Also, as the process was a first, there was a high degree of uncertainty and discomfort. There was a measure of resentment from her peers, seeing Hannah in a lead role, and her seniors did not want to be there!

Her approach, as said earlier, was an outstanding success. The reason it was a success was that Hannah had managed to reverse all the negative factors that cause us to wish we were anywhere except at the meeting we are attending.

What are the critical questions?

In summary, the critical questions that Hannah answered were, from the perspective of a member of a meeting:

- Why are we holding this meeting?
- What do we expect to achieve as a result of the meeting?
- Why am I attending?
- What is expected of me?
- How shall I be able to make an effective contribution?
- What kind of chairperson shall we have and how will she or he run the meeting?
- How long will it last?
- What shall I have to do as a result of the meeting?

Now the process Hannah devised and applied is not going to be appropriate for all meetings, nor when we have a leadership role and need to be a contributor to the debate. However, at the heart of effective meetings is, as to be expected, the effective interaction of a small group of people, that enables the discovery of better solutions to problems than would have been the case if individuals had considered the problems on their own.

To achieve this, the chairperson needs to ensure that there is involvement in setting the agenda, a clear picture of the reason for the meeting given, and a process set out and agreed that enables the interactions of the group to be effective—within the agreed timetable.

In short, the chairperson is not a controller of people but of process.

How to hold effective interviews

What this chapter covers

Here we look at how to improve our interviewing skills, taking as the example the job or promotion interview, where we are taking or contributing to the decision that a particular candidate should be employed, promoted, or passed on to a high-fliers' programme. We might be from personnel, we might be an executive on a career development or recruitment panel, or a manager interviewing an internal or external candidate to be one of our team members.

We look first at the key actions required to carry out an effective interview, then exemplify them by looking at part of an interview, concluding by consideration of what were the right questions that enabled us to be effective.

Key actions

How do you ensure that you carry out an effective interview? What are the key actions you should take?

Re-write the job description—identify the critical skills you can assess

Professor Drucker once said that one defect that many interviewers suffered was that they identified and focused on weaknesses rather than identifying and focusing on the key strengths or skills needed to perform the job well. He saw it as a Western cultural mindset—a natural tendency to criticize than praise. To criticize effectively, weaknesses have to be uncovered. The result was that some candidates, who would perform well, never made the grade and those with limited ability, but without any perceived weaknesses, were employed.

So the first step to being an effective interviewer is to re-write the job description to identify the essential strengths required to carry out the job well, and then, to use your effective questioning and listening skills to assess how well the candidate measures up.

Referring to the section on creativity, it is good idea to write those skills in the forms of actions. This enables them to be assessed in the interview. For example: the ideal candidate can:

- identify the key messages from complex data;
- make quality decisions under stressful conditions;
- build an effective team;
- communicate effectively with clients;
- influence and persuade without authority.

Unless you take this critical first step, you will be 'batting on a very sticky wicket'. Both internal and external job descriptions usually list many qualities that cannot be assessed in an interview (e.g. must display the highest integrity), often have a lot of detail about role and responsibilities rather than key strengths or actions required, occasionally have attributes that are mutually exclusive (e.g. must be a decisive leader … must be a team player) and usually lead one to believe that only a close relative of God should apply!

Incidentally, knowledge is usually an entry barrier to the interview, i.e. only candidates who have passed the knowledge criteria are coming under your scrutiny, which is why you can focus on skill.

Leave other evidence until after the interview

External and internal candidates are increasingly being asked to complete a battery of psychometrics, and the interviewer has the results at his or her disposal. A wise interviewer uses them to confirm his or her judgement after the interview and not to develop a mindset before. Otherwise you may be tough on one whose personality is not quite right (or a bit different from your own?) and lenient on one who passes muster.

You cannot assess personality very easily or objectively (which is why the tests have been filled in), but you can judge competence to do the job. So discipline yourself not to look at the results until you have had your effective interview—a necessary precursor to which is to have an open and objective mind.

Be prepared for interviewee 'tricks'

I have come across many successful interviewees, who pulled the wool over the interviewer's eyes. They opened the interviewer up with their own skilful questioning, listened attentively, agreed appropriately, embellished with their own stories, displaying just how much they were on the same wavelength as the interviewer, and left with a smile on their face and the job in their pocket.

The interviewer was fulsome in praise of such a candidate, though often short of a few objective reasons why this was the outstanding candidate. They were not difficult to find, such was the enthusiasm for the one right answer!

Obey the 80/20 rule

This follows from the last point. A useful rule of thumb is that you should only speak for around 20 per cent of the time and the interviewee around 80 per cent. In fact, I would suggest that, with your powerful open questioning approach, you could aim for an even lower percentage of the conversation. One of the advantages of having identified a clear set of skills in advance is that it will help immensely to ensure (a) that you focus on each skill as the heart of the interview and force yourself to question and listen and (b) that the other party answers and reveals all that you need to know to make your decision.

Be objective

Remember, you are in questioning and listening mode. An interview is not an attempt to develop an effective relationship with the interviewee, which is another reason why you must avoid all attempts by the clever interviewee to question you and leave you with that warm glow. The job interview has the simple objective of enabling you to objectively assess the competence of the interviewee to meet the key skills required to do the job well.

Clearly you need to set the interviewee at ease, part of the next point, to ensure that the probes are answered—but this is an occasion of cool professionalism and suspended judgement throughout. To be an effective interviewer imposes a discipline of thought and attitude that is difficult to achieve. However, with well-developed questioning and listening skills, and a clear structure or agenda, those difficulties will disappear.

Use structure to control the interview

It is important to allow yourself a few minutes, not only to re-write the job description, but also to determine the structure you want to follow. Once that is in place, you can then control the interview from beginning to end. An approach that works well consists of four phases:

1. Social chit chat—setting the interviewee at ease.

2. Setting and agreeing the objective. (By this I mean that you advise the interviewee that the job requires certain key skills to be performed well and you intend to determine how competent he or she is in those skills, check if that is OK (which it will be—verbally at least!) and then you will be happy to answer any questions that the interviewee has about the job or any other matters of concern.)

3. Outline and assess competence in each skill.

4. Answer all questions.

Incidentally, your professional and objective approach will be welcomed by good candidates and put others off their stride.

Focus on examples and situations

Well, you are an old hand at effective questioning now, and will appreciate that asking someone if they can take tough decisions under stressful conditions is likely to produce a 'Yes', which does not take you very much further forward!. You need to probe by asking for examples and situations and then probe their answers even further, until they have revealed exactly what you need to know to make your judgement.

Take notes

It is unwise to rely on memory, and so discipline yourself to take notes, having asked for permission, which will be granted.

Assessing skills

We conclude this chapter with the key part of an actual interview, focused on assessing skills. We shall assume that one skill identified as a key to effective performance in the job is the ability to take tough decisions under stressful conditions.

Linda: Well, Charles, as head of sales you will need to make some tough decisions under stressful conditions. For instance, you may need to change the sales mix and focus, gear up very quickly to push a new product line, or, if one product line fails or becomes a 'dog', pull out quickly and perhaps lay off sales staff. It is always tough at the top. So, tell me, Charles, when did you last face what, looking back, was a tough decision in stressful conditions?

Charles: Funny you should ask that one, Linda. Only six months ago, I had to face one of the decisions you have already identified. One of our major product lines began to falter and then sales dropped like the proverbial stone, before settling down at less than half the initial volumes. This meant we had to cut costs and where else but staff, the biggest cost of all?

Linda just paused and looked interested.

[*This is where discipline comes in. You are not there to have a dialogue where you promote discovery—but to probe and probe again. So resist the temptation to ask any questions about other options that could have been taken apart from matching sales staff reduction to market share loss.*]

Charles: So I had to let go over half the sales force in pretty short order.
Linda: When you say you had to let go, was it your decision alone?
Charles: Oh! yes. Senior managers like me are expected to take tough decisions, and not involve the Board. I did get the nod from my boss, of course, as a matter of courtesy.
Linda: I see. And how did you set about implementing the decision?
Charles: Oh! that was fairly easy. There were only 16 sales staff involved and three managers—19 in all. We aimed for a total of nine, and used the opportunity to restructure so that there was only one manager, who had eight direct reports. I knew them all pretty well and with Personnel providing additional data from staff reports, it was easy to identify who should go and who should stay.
Linda: So who communicated the decision to those staff, who were going?
Charles: Well, I know of senior managers, who pass the buck to Personnel. Not me, I know my responsibilities. I told them the bad news.
Linda: And how did you communicate the news to them?
Charles: Having agreed the list and the terms we would provide, it was simply a matter of a day of painful interviews with the 10 we were letting go. I saw each individual for about half-an-hour—gave it to them straight from the shoulder, no other way really, explained when they would actually leave, what the financial terms were and gave them a name in Personnel for further counselling and support.
Linda: And how was morale in the salesforce that remained?
Charles: Took a bit of a knock for a few months afterwards—inevitable I suppose, but then picked up slowly and we recovered to around the same sales to staff ratio that we were at before the whole incident.

Analysis

When Linda looks at her notes afterwards and reflects on the answers provided, she will find that she has all the information she needs to make a judgement.

On the one hand, Charles find these decisions rather easy, does not have a very caring approach, did not involve staff at all in exploring alternatives to being sacked (which some decision takers have done with outstanding success), and failed to demonstrate any decisions he took in positively intervening as a leader to improve the morale of staff who stayed on; nor for that matter did he make any reference to the sole manager, left in an isolated position, with extra responsibilities.

On the other hand, he was decisive—he did not dither, nor did he shirk his responsibilities of personally informing his staff. He was a business-focused, decisive individual. Linda will know whether, in this area, Charles's approach to decision making is what the company requires.

Linda disciplined herself to remain objective and not get involved, obeyed the 80/20 rule, asked one closed question (to establish a fact) and five open questions.

- When did you face a tough decision in stressful conditions? (The follow-up 'And what exactly was the decision?' was unnecessary, as Charles answered it without it being asked.)
- How did you set about implementing the decision? 'Probing' how (the 'probing' what was implicit and preceded this).
- Who communicated the decision? (Asking for relevant information.)
- How did you communicate the news to them? (Further probing.)
- How was the morale in the salesforce that remained? Further probing, and giving Charles the opportunity not just to reply but to indicate how he improved morale, which he failed to take.

Charles may have been decisive, but was not much of a strategic thinker.

Part III
DEVELOPING KEY RELATIONSHIPS

How to relate effectively with the boss

What this chapter covers

In this chapter we consider why the relationship with the boss is important, what can stop us having an effective relationship and how to ensure that we have a quality relationship—i.e. determining the actions we should take. Again we shall use relevant conversations and analyse appropriate questioning approaches to demonstrate key points made.

Why the boss is important

There are two key reasons why it is in our interest as 'subordinates' or 'followers' or 'direct reports' to have an effective relationship with our boss or, in these days of matrix management, with our bosses.

To improve our career

If our boss becomes our champion in the organization for which we work, then he or she will be doing everything possible to ensure that we get any promotions that are available or can be created and, just as importantly in these days of 'downsizing' or 'rightsizing', ensure that we survive when others fall by the wayside. It is not always the most able who stay or the least able who go.

To improve our performance

If we have a boss who gives us guidance when we want guidance, who gives us support when we want support, and open doors for us in the organization when we need doors opened, we shall be more effective in our performance—in doing the job we are paid to do.

What gets in the way of a good relationship?

We shall look at two general reasons that can inhibit an effective relationship with other aspects covered in the final section: 'How to improve our relationship with the boss.' The first barrier is a combination of psychological attitude and sheer ignorance or lack of perception, and the second covers the critical area of 'organizational politics' or culture. In each case we accentuate the positive.

We need to change our mindsets

Many, if not nearly all, of us can develop a negative attitude to bosses for three generic reasons, which we shall consider in turn.

Do not think of a boss as a 'boss'

If we look in a dictionary for the definition of the noun 'boss', we find 'master, person in authority, overseer'. If we look at the verb we find: 'be master or manager of, give orders to'. Finally, to boss about is defined as 'continually give peremptory orders to'.

The word boss and its literal meaning of 'someone in authority over us, who has the right to order us about' is deeply embedded in our subconscious. There are times—perhaps when new to a job or when much change is happening—when we certainly need guidance, i.e. to be provided with a sense of direction. Most of the time, however, as we develop our confidence and competence—build our self-esteem—the last thing we want is the literal 'boss'.

So, irrelevant of the actual personality of the boss (I shall continue with the word as it is so universal in its usage), a boss gets off to a bad start as there is an instinctive resistance to having a boss in the first place!

We therefore need to think of a boss as someone else. A leader is a better word, but this still conjures up feelings of being 'subordinate' and 'being told'. You choose. But a good word, if you want to achieve the two key benefits of career improvement and better job competence, is 'facilitator'—someone who, with your effective questioning and relationship management skills, will help you achieve what you want to achieve.

Remember your boss goes to work to do a good job

We all have conversations we forget, and we all have conversations, few and far between, that we always remember because they provided significant meaning or value to us. A few years ago I was speaking to a consultant, from a large consulting firm, who had spent all his working life

(30 years at the time of the conversation) in the international arena—in fact the only part of the world where he had not worked was South America. So I asked him, given his exposure to so many different cultures and races, what were the commonalties between the different cultures. He replied that there were three:

1. *The differences between cultures were not as great as the individual culture perceived.* Many people develop personal identity by being part of a wider community. There is a natural tendency to accentuate difference to develop identity, and often a desire to see one's own culture as superior to others—to develop self-esteem. If taken to extreme, relationships between cultures break down. Too often, we fail to recognize the common bond of humanity we all share. Valuing difference through recognizing commonality is a powerful way of creating value and not discord from the smaller differences that emerge.

2. *Everyone goes to work to do a good job.* We go to work to do a good job. So do our bosses. I have met many managers who believe that their bosses go to work to do a bad job and achieve their objective!

3. *Everyone wants to improve his or her circumstances.* All people want to develop something for themselves/their families/communities— whether it is better standard of living, a better quality of life and so on.

Recognize the existence and impact of perception gaps

Picking up on 'Everyone goes to work to do a good job', bosses have good intentions, as we do, but their actual behavioural manifestation of those intentions can be different from the intention, and, even if it is not, the actual impact on us can be different. We shall develop this theme in the next chapter, when we look at our relationship with a 'follower' or 'direct report'.

As followers, we should remember that bosses may, from our perception, be behaving badly—criticizing less than constructively, sending out a memo detailing changes we should make, or interrupting us to 'make a helpful suggestion'. From their perception they are giving us support, providing guidance or helping us succeed at our jobs!

Do you believe me?

It's absolutely true and if you are going to have an effective relationship with your boss, you must recognize that bosses don't intend to behave as badly as they may do from your perception. (You might, of course, have a perfect relationship with your boss. If you do, you are the exception.) I shall illustrate this by two true stories, rolled into one as the conversations with the bosses and one direct report of each boss were almost identical. In one instance, the boss was the group finance director of a multinational travel services company (and the direct report was a finance director); in the other, the boss was a main board director and chief executive officer of a manufacturing subsidiary, and the direct report was his marketing director.

Looking first at the conversation with the boss, with Q standing for questioner and B for boss, we have:

Q: So, how would you describe your leadership style?

B: Well, I think I would say I was an empowering leader, who trusted his staff.

Q: An empowering, trusting leader—very powerful. How do you demonstrate this leadership approach?

B: Well, it's simple really. Let us say, a project crosses my desk which I have neither the time nor the inclination to handle personally. I shall call the appropriate person in, or, to be honest, most of the time whoever is available, as we are all so busy these days, and I say: 'I trust you and I empower you. Here's this little project for you to do. I know you will do an excellent job—best of luck, or some such thing.' And what is more, usually a few days later, I have some spare time on my hands, so I pop along to help that person with the project.

Now to the follower's (A's) perspective:

Q: So, how you would describe the kind of leadership you receive?

A: My boss is a dictator. [*The other follower used the word 'tyrant'.*]

Q: Oh! dear. How does he demonstrate this dictatorial approach?

A: Well, you know how overworked I am, with my increased responsibilities and number of direct reports. Well, in the midst of trying to cope, I get the dreaded summons to the boss's office. Then I hear the two words I hate most in the English language— 'empower' and 'trust'. He waffles on about how he trusts me and is going to empower me—then dumps on me some God awful project, which I haven't time to do, and sometimes, haven't got the technical skill. Then he dismisses me with words like 'I know you'll do a good job'.

Well, what do I do? I either dump it down, 'sorry—empower one of my staff!' or, more often than not, as my staff are working all hours like me, I try my best to do the job. What is even worse is that a few days later, he saunters into my office, asks how I am getting on, reviews what I have done, and points out all my mistakes!

Part of the function of an effective follower is to reduce or eliminate those perception gaps through effective questioning, examined in the final section 'How to improve our relationship with the boss'.

On the questioning side, only open questions were used: two in each conversation and all 'probing' hows. Also, in the first case there was some reflection and, in the second, a little bit of empathy.

Let us now turn to the second barrier to a good relationship.

We need to understand there is a game to be played

I shall illustrate what exactly I mean by using the example of a conversation, based on a real-life situation of an up-and-coming high flier, Mary, working as an assistant manager in market research, whose boss, Harry, is head of research. Harry's boss in turn is Lena, the head of the marketing department, and her boss is the sales and marketing director, Arnold.

Mary had done a few ad hoc projects for Arnold directly, initially because she was the first person Arnold had got hold of, and subsequently, because Mary had done excellent work the first time round. **EXAMPLE**

Arnold had just finished briefing Mary on another little project. Then, out of the blue, as Mary was about to leave, he said: 'I like you, Mary—you remind me of how I was 25 years ago, apart from the gender difference, of course. So, I am going to give you some sound advice, which I suggest you listen to and follow.'

'Oh, thank you, Arnold. Of course, I will', said Mary.

'Now, you believe, don't you Mary, that if you perform very well you will be promoted, and that if you continue to perform well and exceed what this organization expects of you, you will continue to be promoted. In other words, you believe that good performance is the key to a successful career?', Arnold asked.

'I do, indeed Arnold.'

'And why do you believe that, Mary?'

'Because that is what I have been told, Arnold—what is more, the appraisal system is structured to measure and reward performance. And also, that has been my experience. To date, I have performed very well, and I have been promoted.'

'I see, Mary, that is a bit of a worry. You may be right in the early days of your career, when you are still junior, but those days are over. You are now completely wrong, and I want you to understand this so that you have the effective career your talents deserve', remarked Arnold.

'Well, I hear what you say, Arnold, but I am afraid that I do not really understand why you say what you say.'

'I know, Mary', Arnold commented. 'Let me explain. Every organization has a culture, the way things are done round here, if you like. There are always two sides to the cultural coin—the light side and the dark side. You are operating at the moment purely in the light side. Unless you learn to walk in the shadows—in the twilight zone of the culture, you will fail in your career ambitions.'

'I see, Arnold', said Mary. In fact, she didn't see anything at all! She was in her own little twilight zone. 'Could you be more specific, please?'

Arnold chuckled at Mary's obvious discomfiture. 'The twilight zone is all to do with human nature and particularly its frailties. If you like, the explicit or light side is where our hopes and aspirations lie. The implicit or dark side is where our less noble natures express themselves. For instance, on the light side, we might say and believe that feedback is good and so we say that we encourage an open, honest atmosphere of two-way feedback between the boss and subordinate.

'On the dark side, where reality not aspiration lies, if a subordinate were to directly criticize her boss, who might be directly criticizing her all the time, she would probably destroy her career. Bosses don't take kindly to criticism from a subordinate. If it became a habit, the boss might not tell the subordinate off, as he might not like direct confrontation. What he would do, almost inevitably, is ensure the subordinate's appraisal did not reflect her actual performance, and he would be very lukewarm indeed in supporting her when it came to promotion.

'Take another of so many examples. These days, we promote creative thinking, as our industry is at the forefront of change, and ideas help us to manage change effectively. So we encourage ideas on the light side of the culture, but not on the dark side, especially from juniors like yourself, unless they are purely focused on completing the task that you have been given, or unless you are asked to come up with ideas, which hardly ever happens.

'On the dark side, if a subordinate were to suggest to her boss that he takes on board a good idea she has, then he might well think that she was criticizing the way he does things. Now the boss is responsible for the status quo, with which he will personally identify. An idea necessarily suggests a difference to the status quo. So, by expressing an idea, the subordinate could be and often will be seen by many bosses as criticizing them even though that is not the intention. So, the subordinate has fallen into the dangerous trap, by coming up with an idea, of criticizing the boss—not a career progressive move.

'Do you begin to understand, Mary?'

'Yes, Arnold, I am beginning to see the light, or is it the dark?'

'I'll forgive that attempt at humour,' Arnold replied. 'Let me make it more personal. You have done some excellent work for me recently, and I bet you think that it has enhanced your career prospects. In fact, you may well have been boasting a bit to your colleagues about this?'

Mary looked a little bit sheepish, but said nothing.

'You couldn't be more wrong, I'm afraid. Unwittingly, I have done you a disservice. Let me ask you a few questions. Did you consult with Harry and ask for his input and advice before giving anything to me, having clearly briefed him on what I wanted you to do and why?'

'No, I didn't', said Mary. 'Though a few times he was not around.'

'But you could have written to Harry, and kept him informed that way, could you not?' Arnold continue probing.

'I could have, but I didn't because I didn't see the need.'

'OK. Did you brief him afterwards, feedback the results of our meetings?' asked Arnold.

'No, I did not', replied Mary.

'Well, look at it from Harry's point of view and my point of view. You are so far removed from me that I do not take decisions on your career. If I were to take decisions at your level, I would spend almost all my time doing that. That is not my job. My job is to ensure that the sales division meets its targets, and help steer, together with my colleagues on the board, the corporate ship to a safe harbour.'

'Of course, I understand that', acknowledged Mary.

'Now your boss, Harry, knows all about the twilight zone. It is important that he pleases Lena, and he is very keen to make a good impression with me. Harry is one step closer to me than you. So I have a little bit more impact on his career. More importantly, if I like him and think he is sound, I might drop that piece of information to the Personnel director when we are chatting, as we often do. Even more importantly, he is due for promotion, and if he gets Lena's job (and Lena, as you know, retires at the end of the year), then I become his boss, and therefore a very important person indeed.'

'I understand that, Arnold.'

'Now how do you think Harry feels about your activities? He sees you getting much more direct access to me than he does, he sees you in my confidence when he is not, and he sees you keeping him in the dark completely, and, for all he knows, deliberately.'

'Harry is going to be one unhappy man', Mary said ruefully.

'And who is Harry going to blame for this highly negative state of affairs? Me, a very important person in his eyes, or you, a very unimportant person in his eyes?'

'Well, me of course. But why hasn't he spoken to me?' asked Mary.

Arnold laughed uproariously. 'There is one golden rule of the twilight zone. No one ever speaks about it. You only learn the hard way. Good God woman, do you know anyone who would deliberately and openly say such things as "I'm an insecure, petty, jealous person, who resents you for what you are doing, even though it is not your fault"? Enough, Mary, here endeth your first and I would imagine your last lesson on the twilight zone.'

The game can be called 'walking in the twilight zone' or 'dealing with office politics' or 'understanding human nature'. It does not matter what it is called, but I have seen the careers of many good women and men destroyed or their jobs lost because they did not know there was a game to be played. If you are just a pawn in a game of chess, you will be the first to be sacrificed!

Having recognized that bosses are human, like us, and full of the same positive and negative emotions and behaviours that we experience and display, let us turn to the final section—the 'dos' and 'don'ts' of having an effective relationship with the boss.

How to improve our relationship with the boss

There are eight strategies that you should consider.

Develop a positive attitude to your boss

We have considered this earlier in the section on 'What gets in the way of a good relationship?' If we remember, however awful we may think our boss is, that all bosses:

- should be considered potential allies or facilitators to help us improve our careers and job performance;
- do their best in often trying circumstances;
- do not realize that their good intentions often fall on stony ground

then we shall develop the right attitude or frame of mind towards our boss, without which a quality relationship cannot be developed. We must respect our bosses as the precursor to getting them to respect us, from which base of mutuality an effective relationship will flower.

Never criticize your boss

As we now know, people who are suddenly criticized will immediately descend down the reaction curve, unless they know how to use the assertive pause technique, which hardly anyone does. They will be angry with the source of the criticism, whether or not they reject it or accept it with consequent dent to self-esteem. We all know the phrase 'Kill the messenger'; so don't ever put yourself in a situation where you will be 'killed'.

Nor is it wise to get rid of unresolved frustrations with your boss by making criticisms behind his or her back, because in most cultures, the grapevine will work to your disadvantage, and it will get back to the boss.

If you can create a relationship where you can promote discovery, that is great.

Keep your boss informed

We have already seen the consequences of not keeping the boss in the picture, when it should have been recognized how important it was to do so.

Apply the PBA rule

We have covered this. If you want to communicate effectively with your boss—don't be driven by your logic and your value system. Recognize the boss's value system, what makes him or her tick, and communicate inside the boss's world and not from outside—i.e. inside your world. The more you communicate effectively, the more the worlds will merge.

Bring your boss solutions not problems

Bosses can be very harassed individuals and many genuinely want to help and support their 'subordinates'. So they use such expressions as: 'If you have any problems at all, please come to me and we will sort something out.'

And, like stupid fools, we believe them! You should listen to such bosses when they in a friendly environment, talking about their subordinates. 'It's a nightmare. I try to get some work done, I feel it is vital to keep an open door policy—and I never get any work done, because my subordinates are always coming to me with their problems, many of which are trivial, and they should have resolved themselves, and many should have been sorted out by one of my colleagues—but they keep coming to me.'

And what do we say to such bosses. 'Have a closed door policy one afternoon a week—where possible the same day, and let everyone know what you are doing, why and when. And another thing: encourage your subordinates to bring you solutions not problems.' If you do bring them a problem, good bosses will use very probing questions to get you to work out the answers for yourself. However, that can be quite uncomfortable.

So you should, as a matter of course, go to your boss if you have some important problems—but you do it in a proactive and positive way: 'Thanks for seeing me, Joanna. This problem has just cropped up, and we need to resolve it quickly. Some of the options I have thought up are A, B, C—I'd value your view of things and how we can best take things forward.'

This leads neatly to the next point.

Promote discovery with your boss

As we know, the heart of any effective relationship is where there is mutual problem-solving/situation improvement/opportunity creation. This holds for any relationship—whether peer, subordinate or boss.

Wait for the first reminder

Now this might seem as a bit of an odd-ball suggestion. It isn't. Many years ago, I became involved in lecturing on time management, and read a few books to enable me to put across some relevant points. One very memorable concept was the elephant and the ants.

Elephants represent our key accountabilities—and any job can be broken down to a few key accountabilities (never more than six) for example: increase sales, develop staff and monitor competitors. Each key accountability can be defined by a number of SMART objectives (Set, Measurable, Achievable, Realistic and Timed), and each objective can be broken down into an action plan. So elephants can be sliced, and gobbling up these slices, should be the focus of our job—as it means we will do what we are paid to do—efficiently and effectively.

However, our life is also full of ants—trivial, unimportant work activities. So to be able to concentrate on elephant hunting, we require an ant-elimination policy. Some ways are delegating, grouping and developing systems to manage them. Another is to ignore them—*wait for the first reminder!*

When I learned about this, I thought I would apply it—so I did. I set up an ant-elimination file, and all sorts of junk went into it—questionnaires, requests from head office and some of the things my boss asked me to do!

No real risk really, because, if it was important, I would get a reminder and could get onto it 'straightaway', pleading pressure of work as an excuse. I have never had to. Every six months, I clean out my file. I recall having lunch with the CEO once, who asked me to do a research paper on IBM's approach to training—specifically how they were penetrating the external marketplace. I said 'Yes, of course', and had I done it, it would have been very, very time-consuming. But I am still waiting for the first reminder. He asked me four years ago!

Clearly, you have to use judgement to ensure that you only ignore your boss's 'ants' so that the first reminder hardly ever happens!

Always ask the right question in the right way

We have seen a couple of examples of how to use powerful open questions to ensure that we are seen to be effective followers and our boss becomes a more effective leader. Specifically the first cameo of Chapter 1, where John agreed with the logic of the decision and gained Charles a stay of execution of the move to sales. Then the even more powerful example in Chapter 4, where Harry, the consultant, saved his job by first recognizing his boss's rights and position, before asserting his own, and being proactive in putting forward a viable solution to the problem.

How to relate effectively with a subordinate

What this chapter covers

How effective our relationship is with our 'subordinates', 'followers' or 'direct reports' has a direct bearing on how effective we are in our jobs. If they are motivated and highly competent, they will produce excellent results for us, we shall be perceived as effective leaders, and shall have to work less hard to achieve the goals and targets set for the team we lead (assuming we have more than one direct report).

To develop an effective relationship with a direct report, we must understand exactly what is required of us as leaders—what we have to focus on to develop the relationship.

To start with, we look at what an effective leader does, then consider perception gaps in communication with followers and how to eliminate them. Finally, we focus on one of the best times to develop the relationship—the annual appraisal.

What an effective leader does

If you ask groups of managers or leaders to think of themselves in their 'followership' role and consider what they, earlier in their careers, wanted from their leaders and why, a common picture emerges, whatever the company or country. What is more they recognize that what they want as followers they should deliver as leaders.

So, in this section, I do not distil my views but the views of a group of managers, who happened to be senior managers, working for a multinational company in Malaysia.

Think about the leadership role

There are two aspects to this. If we have a leadership role, we can spend significant amounts of time at work carrying it out whether in written, telephone or face-to-face communication with individual followers or teams of followers. How much of our thinking time do we spend developing and applying a strategy to be effective leaders? Not a lot, for the vast majority. We spend our thinking time, working out how to solve all the problems that beset us, and how to complete all the projects and tasks we undertake. Inasmuch as followers come into our thinking, it is much more how we can manage them rather than lead them.

The other aspect is: Have we determined our fundamental leadership role? Until we do, we are very unlikely to be effective. What happens for many managers in different companies and across many cultures is that they automatically follow the conventional and subconscious view of leadership. (We have touched on this in the previous chapter.) We think, in the main, that our core role is to give the lead! We have to take the touch decisions, the buck stops here, and our followers should come to us for guidance. What is more, this conventional view is accepted by most followers. Time after time, when we nominate one of a group of managers from different companies, who are peers, to be the leader of a particular exercise, the 'followers' start saying things like 'Over to you boss—you take the decision', and the leader responds by doing so.

That view of leadership as an effective way of managing people rapidly changes as the result of failure.

Another view of leadership is emerging and is encapsulated by a quote by Brian Edwards, the managing director of a large printing company, made when reviewing an exercise: 'The effective leader or coach provides motivation on a voyage of discovery where common sense prevails.' This view of leadership emphasizes the role of leader as developer, motivater and coach. My view is much more in tune with Brian Edwards than with the conventional view.

If the fundamental objective of a leader is to maximize the efficiency and effectiveness of those being led (getting the best results through others), then that objective will be achieved if the leader focuses on building effective teams—synergistic, discovery units. Once built, he or she focuses on maintaining those teams at peak performance. That view of the core leadership role is predicated on the fact that the effective team is the best unit to maximize discovery (necessary in a world of change) and provides the most powerful and effective learning for the individual.

For those of you interested in learning how to build and maintain an effective team, I would recommend either my Sunday Times Business Skills Series book *Building your Team* (Kogan Page, 1995) or my book in the Industrial Society Series of 'How to' books, *How to be a Better Team-Builder* (Kogan Page, 1996).

Whatever your view of the core purpose of leadership, the point managers make is that one has to form a view—to think about what the leadership role is and how it can be achieved. Every leader should develop and implement a strategy for effective leadership.

Develop self-awareness and self-belief

Poor leaders display an excess of control, usually because they either need to control or want to control. Debate focused in this instance on need, which was perceived as arising fundamentally from uncertainty. The identified sources of uncertainty were the individuals themselves and/or changes in the business environment. A lack of security and self-belief could be subconscious and, therefore, difficult to deal with owing to lack of recognition.

Good leaders develop an awareness of self. They identify, acknowledge and understand their strengths and weaknesses, believe in themselves and in their competence and capability. Leaders have to think positively about themselves, before they can think positively about those they lead.

The more they are in control of themselves, the less they need to control others.

Focus externally: listen, support, provide feedback and coach

Poor leaders focus on themselves. By developing self-awareness and self-belief, and by becoming comfortable with themselves, good leaders could do what those being led wanted—focus on the follower.

Good leaders are good listeners, providing support at both the logical and emotional levels. They provide feedback (not criticism—see final section) to encourage their followers and enable them to develop. Good leaders are good coaches—they ask the awkward questions that enable the followers to discover and learn for themselves rather than being told what to do.

Display integrity in decision taking and take decisions

Some poor leaders take bad and inconsistent decisions to accommodate the changing power shifts in the body politic or the changing views of those in command. Others take no decisions and 'delegate' them down by default to avoid offending anyone adversely affected by the decision.

Share information

Jan Carlson of Scandinavian Airlines made the remark that: 'An individual without information cannot take responsibility: an individual with information cannot help but take responsibility.'

Good leaders recognize that their followers want responsibility and so share information. They operate a 'need to know' policy from the followers' and not the organizational perspective. They are successful as their followers trust and respect them, and so do not break any confidences. In short, they empower their followers.

Be confident enough to make mistakes, admit mistakes and learn from mistakes

Poor leaders deny learning and effective problem solving to themselves and their followers, because they need to be perceived as infallible.

The word *confidence* was first used here by the Malaysian Senior Managers. That is the outcome of self-awareness and self-belief, allied with the humility to recognize that capability does not mean infallibility, and that change requires continuous learning.

Direct with coaching

This point recognizes that, as we know, there are occasions when any manager or executive needs direction or guidance—when there is a crisis, or they are in an unfamiliar role or handling a new task beyond current capability. The 'with coaching' part reflects the desire for a shared process of discovery with the 'how', having been provided with the 'what' and 'why'.

Delegate authority as well as responsibility

An effective leaders knows when to hand over the reins, as well as the horse! From the followers' perspective, if their leader is confident and capable, listens, supports, provides feedback and coaching, shares his or her thoughts, ideas and other information, is there to take the tough decisions when needed, to provide guidance when the follower is uncertain and insecure, yet gives the follower the reins when he or she has developed confidence, then that follower would be a very contented person—and what is more, the leader would produce optimal business results from him or her.

How to eliminate perception gaps

We have already introduced perception gaps from the perspective of the follower. Now we need to look at how they arise and how they can be eliminated. Please refer to Figure 10.1, 'How perception gaps arise'.

You will notice that there are two gaps—the gap between conscious intent and manifestation (gap 1) and the gap between manifestation and the impact on the other party (gap 2), in this instance the follower.

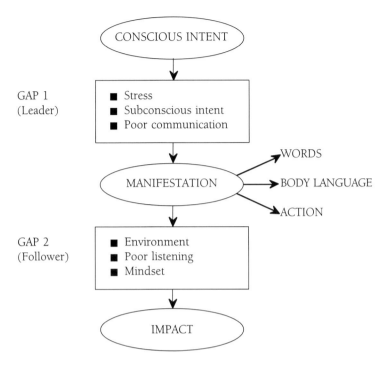

Figure 10.1 *How perception gaps arise.*

As an example, we shall take a situation where we want to persuade a colleague to change the way she is managing a project.

Our conscious motivation or intent is to transfer a little of our expertise to Sally, say, so that she does the project better. We assume that we are her boss, and are accountable for the results of the project—so there is an element of self-interest. We will also assume that she is the project leader and we hold only a watching brief. She has been given both the authority and responsibility to manage the project team.

No gaps arise in the right environment with the right approach. Let us say that the words we use, with consistent non-verbal signals or 'body language', are: 'I have got a good idea on how we can reduce the time taken to install the new network.'

Now:

- if this suggestion comes as part of a regular weekly review of the project with Sally;
- there is an agenda, where key aspects of the project are discussed;
- information technology (IT) is the item being discussed

then, provided our idea is sound, it is likely to be gratefully accepted. There are no gaps. The suggestion is part and parcel of explicit expectations set, and phrased in a positive non-critical way. Because the behavioural manifestation expresses the intent effectively, there is no gap 1. With the environment also right, there is no gap 2. We achieve our objective, which is to get Sally to 'change'—to do something differently from what she would have done without our effective intervention.

It is accepted because we have created an environment where there is 'shared voyage of discovery'. Sally will be coming through with her ideas, as well, and both parties will be developing ideas together.

In the wrong environment, though there is no gap 1, we may cause a gap 2. We shall return to this when we look at gap 2. We now focus on the causes of gap 1.

How the gap between intention and behavioural manifestation arises

We shall look at each cause in turn.

We are under stress

We may be under stress, feeling irritable, in a rush and so on. So we say: 'The installation time for the new network can be reduced by 50 per cent. This is what you have to do....' Interestingly, when under stress or in a rush, when we are feeling the pressure, there is a natural inclination to move into a more 'tell style' or 'command and control' leadership approach. As we have seen, the problem with that is that some staff will only verbally agree and ignore us afterwards, and others will do their level best to implement our suggestions or 'instructions', but do not fully understand or 'own' the solution and will implement them imperfectly.

In fact, we may well not bother with a face-to-face meeting, and send a written communication to Sally, advising her of what to do to improve the management of *her* project. Putting yourself in Sally's shoes, would you see that intervention as a helpful suggestion, which acknowledges and respects her authority and competence as project leader? Yet that was the intent!

Incidentally, there are many executives, who use written instruction as a matter of course, with no intention to upset or demotivate and no knowledge that that is the impact—because the follower is not prepared to volunteer feedback, which is never requested. In any case, if feedback is ever 'requested', it will never be honest. If the employee is on the way out, honest feedback may be volunteered and ignored!

We are driven by the subconscious

A positive conscious intention may hide a subconscious or implicit intention that is more negative. So our conscious desire may be to improve the position, but to build self-esteem, we also want to criticize. The way we behave manifests such hidden intentions.

> 'Sally, your plan to install the new network is flawed. I have come up with a way to reduce installation time by 50 per cent. This is what you have to do....'

Human nature being what it is, Sally is likely to pick the word flaw as the key word in the sentences, and react negatively to what she perceives as implied criticism.

We communicate badly

The third part is simply poor communication. If we are the expert, and know more than Sally on IT matters (perhaps one of her team is the IT expert), then we may use language, jargon, or concepts she does not fully understand. She may perceive us as blinding her with science, or proving our superiority in the chosen area, and none of these perceptions is intended. Unless she acknowledges her lack of understanding and seeks and receives clarification (and often people are reluctant to expose ignorance), then implementation of the change will not be fully effective, or the wrong change will be implemented—neither of which is a desirable outcome.

In summary, if there is a gap 1, the manifestation of intent will produce an impact, necessarily different from the intent. The other person accurately responds to the behaviour manifested, as that is the explicit demonstration of intent. She will assume, because of the gap, an intent that is consistent with the manifestation, but not the initiator's actual intent. Hence the misperception that can be so damaging to relationships and to the effective initiation of change. In this case there is no gap 2.

To close these gap 1 causes:

- We must recognize and try to eliminate stress, at least temporarily. Avoid the hasty memo or sudden intervention by telephone or 'dropping in'. In fact, what will help significantly in terms of our stress and that of the other party, is if we have a policy of proactively managing the environment so that it is conducive to the acceptance of change before we make our intentions known.

- We must deliberately use the 'assertive pause', not this time in reaction but before initiation—consciously consider our intention and motivations and try to identify and eliminate any critical aspects *before* we speak.

■ We must try to avoid jargon, and, as a matter of policy, check that the other party has understood what he or she has agreed to.

How the gap between manifestation and impact arises

While manifestation of intent can match impact, the environment in which the interchange occurs, or the poor listening skills of the receiver or his or her mindset towards the transmitter, means that the actual impact is different from intent/manifestation. We shall look at each in turn.

The leader enters the wrong environment

As already mentioned, the environment in which an interchange takes place is critical to the outcome. So if the message is delivered in a way that is consistent as to intention and manifestation, then the impact can still be negative because the environment is wrong.

Both the leader and the follower have a responsibility to manage the environment proactively. As suggested, the leader should avoid the un-expected, such as dropping by or telephoning with his new idea. The follower also needs to be assertive when the leader is entering the wrong environment, and advise the leader that he or she is busy at a meeting, going to a meeting, and so on.

The follower does not listen

The follower may not have heard the message correctly. There can be cause and effect with the environment, where the listener is distracted by pressure of other work *or* the listener has failed to listen actively, and only focuses on part of the message or misinterprets the message.

This is not a problem, provided the leader does not make assumptions that agreement means understanding, and ensures that those assumptions are checked. We can see however that, in theory, the leader can be considered as not responsible for the causes of gap 2, but needs to be proactive to avoid the harmful effects that can result. It is the price paid for being the initiator if success is desired, or simply the responsibility of an effective leader initiating change.

The follower has a fixed mindset

People will often not believe the evidence of their own eyes. It happens in personal relationships and in business relationships. People come to expect what happened in the past, and pass judgements which become unwritten rules of behaviour towards the other person in the relationship.

They do not notice change in attitude or approach. So, if the followers perceive the initiator of change, their leader, as someone who has in the past criticized when suggesting change or told them what to do out of stress or communicated poorly, i.e. there has always been a gap 1, they may well react to effective communication of intent as if there was still a gap!

This is very difficult for the initiator or leader to respond effectively to. The leader is likely to think: 'Here am I trying to respect Sally's position as project leader, and suggesting a useful change in a positive way, and all she does is throw it back in my face. Well, I am not standing for that. Now, Sally, let me tell you …' He receives an unexpected reaction, perceived negatively, and moves automatically down the reaction curve, into control mode.

You may discover a direct way of handling this situation. All I can suggest is an avoidance strategy. If you, as leader, ensure that the environment is right, that itself will begin to change the perceptions of the person with the negative mindset. Another approach would be to introduce the group discovery technique (GDT), so that one-to-one issues transfer to small group issues, and are solved effectively by the power of the GDT process.

Finally we need to consider the cumulator.

What is the cumulator?

The cumulator is the combination of a cause (or causes) in gap 1 and gap 2. They can combine in an explosive way to lead to the most unfavourable outcome from a shouting match to employee dismissal. For instance, the leader's conscious intention is to make a helpful intervention, but he or she criticizes and the intervention occurs in the wrong environment—in front of the follower's own subordinates. This is not deliberate by the initiator, who has rushed in with a brainwave, but the combination of gaps can produce explosive and damaging outcomes. These problems will be eliminated if the initiator has recognized they can arise and has ensured that the right environment has been created before any exchange.

In the next section we shall discuss the opportunity every leader has to develop an effective relationship with a subordinate—the appraisal—and consider what goes wrong currently, and how appraisals can be transformed.

What goes wrong with appraisals

There are three fundamental problems with many, many appraisal systems.

The wrong goals

The outcome of many appraisal systems is not only a review of performance, but a grade or mark, which determines salary change, level of bonus. Increasingly, organizations are recognizing that performance review should be separated from assessing and rewarding performance, and restating the goal of appraisal as 'to review performance and agree a strategy to improve it'.

The wrong focus

Traditional appraisals reflect the traditional view of leadership. The boss assesses the performance of the follower. There is rarely if ever a real dialogue and discovery, as no mutuality is built into the appraisal process. We cover this point in more detail in the 'How to develop an effective appraisal'.

In such structures, what determines the outcome is the perception of the follower held by the leader, as he or she holds the positional power. I can recall one organization that thought it had cracked the problem by allowing the follower on the form to comment on the appraisal— comments that would be reviewed by the boss's boss.

It was a genuine attempt to improve the situation by the organization, and completely failed. Within nanoseconds, the word went out: 'Never, ever put any negative comment in the new box.' Such comments were guaranteed to be career regressive. When push came to shove, it was always in the interests of a boss to support a direct report in preference to a direct report of a direct report.

Now many companies are experimenting with what they call the 360 degrees appraisal, with very mixed results indeed. In fact, I was talking to a manager on a programme a few weeks ago—and he was in fear for his life as his company had introduced a 360 degrees appraisal. He and three of his colleagues had been asked to appraise their boss, as had two peers and his boss's boss. Anonymity was guaranteed, and the forms sent back directly to Personnel. Unfortunately, everyone thought this guy was a terrible leader, had duly provided that view on the feedback, which had been reported back to the leader, for whom it had come as a terrible, unexpected shock and the grapevine roar was that he was out for revenge!

So much for anonymity!

In any case, as we know, criticism is not the way to improve the performance of any leader!

Lack of skills

Most managers have been provided with little support to ask the right question and listen effectively to the answer.

How to develop an effective appraisal

A number of companies have recognized the drawbacks to conventional or impersonal 360 degrees appraisals and are introducing a new approach, which has the following key features:

- *Separate performance review from reward.* They are introducing a performance improvement system, and not an appraisal system. The reward of money based on performance occurs at a fixed date, after the financial results for the year, whereas the performance improvement meeting is based on the date the job holder started the specific job.

- *Develop a mutuality goal.* The performance of both parties is considered, and not just the subordinate. An example of a goal that enshrines this mutual approach is: 'The purpose of the appraisal is for the performance of each party to be reviewed and each to have agreed an action plan to improve performance.'

- *Identify the key areas on which performance needs to be assessed.* The following shows an example.

  The manager:

  1. Is achieving agreed objectives.
  2. Displays enthusiasm and commitment to achieving agreed objectives.
  3. Has developed the technical knowledge to carry out his/her role effectively.
  4. Has built an effective team.
  5. Manages relationships internally and externally effectively.
  6. Understands and contributes to the strategy for his/her part of the organization.
  7. Has created/used opportunities to work with at least one other division of the organization to achieve a shared goal.

- *Follow a promoting discovery approach.* This requires skill development for most managers, but results in each party asking the other how he or she performed in each competence and to demonstrate his or her view by referring to specific situations and examples. In short, asking the other party to prove any areas of competence and areas for development as well as the actions that are required and the support that is needed to play more effectively to strengths and eradicate those weaknesses that are detrimental to job performance.

■ *Ensure monitoring of action plans.* Monitoring of action plans is best achieved by short, quarterly review meetings.

The power of this approach to 'appraisal' is that it improves the relationship significantly, but with a business focus—so that each helps the other ensure continuous improvement in their business performance.

How to delight your client

What this chapter covers

In this concluding chapter, we consider what should be our goal—what we want from the relationship—and then form a complete model of how to delight a client, from the beginning of the relationship to the achievement of a long-term partnership. The model has been developed as the combination of three sources of information:

1. The research and development required for me to 'lecture' on the subject.

2. The conclusions of numerous conversations with executives and managers from a wide range of companies, industries and countries.

3. Carrying out a sales role in my own organization for the last three years.

The assumption is that you are part of an organization that has a number of different products or services to sell, and that you have a partial or complete selling role. However, many of the approaches suggested will also be helpful if you are a sole trader with a single product or service line.
  I should like to add two further points:

■ To the extent that your organization is moving towards the concept and practice of internal clients, there will be some powerful messages on how to delight such clients, especially if you are a 'boss'.

■ With the progressive contracting out of labour, and the ending of a career for life as the norm, the need to develop effective relationships with customers or clients has never been greater.

Finally, cameos and conversations will be used to illustrate specific points.

What is the goal?

The goal for a successful client relationship is just the same as for all the relationships we have considered—namely, to create an environment where both parties develop new insights and perspectives on problems, which lead to effective action by both parties and the development of a long-term partnership which brings significant added value to both parties.

How to delight a client

Figure 11.1 illustrates a how/how approach. We shall look in turn at the first action at the keyline or second level (e.g. agree needs), followed by actions that support that level (e.g. understand the business/cultural context), and then move to the next action at the keyline (meet needs) and so on in a structured way.

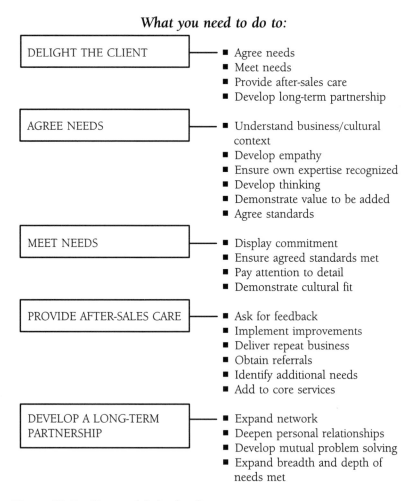

What you need to do to:

DELIGHT THE CLIENT
- Agree needs
- Meet needs
- Provide after-sales care
- Develop long-term partnership

AGREE NEEDS
- Understand business/cultural context
- Develop empathy
- Ensure own expertise recognized
- Develop thinking
- Demonstrate value to be added
- Agree standards

MEET NEEDS
- Display commitment
- Ensure agreed standards met
- Pay attention to detail
- Demonstrate cultural fit

PROVIDE AFTER-SALES CARE
- Ask for feedback
- Implement improvements
- Deliver repeat business
- Obtain referrals
- Identify additional needs
- Add to core services

DEVELOP A LONG-TERM PARTNERSHIP
- Expand network
- Deepen personal relationships
- Develop mutual problem solving
- Expand breadth and depth of needs met

Figure 11.1 *How to delight the client.*

Agree needs

The word 'needs' is critical. We should focus on customer *needs*—which may not be fully appreciated or understood by the customer at the time of initial contact—and not on customer *wants*.

A lot of disservice has been done by the fairly widespread view that the 'customer is king', which has led many organizations to adopt 'client first' schemes. Such schemes, promoted on the light side of the culture, lead to an implicit rule on the dark side 'staff second'. Staff, who are treated as and feel inferior to clients, won't provide effective service to them. 'The customer is king' leads to a drive to please the customers, which in turn leads to non-assertive relationships with customers, where only wants are satisfied. Expectations, based on need, can never be exceeded. In such organizations, the client can never be delighted.

Two cameos, based on real life, will illustrate this fundamental point. It is a continuation of the Tim/John story.

How focus on wants failed

Tim was a little dispirited. He had accepted all the changes imposed from New York, and passed down by his MD, with reasonable grace, but he couldn't stop feeling that a man of his status and position as an executive should no longer have to do any actual selling.

He had made sure that he received the warmest of leads from the tele-sales team, but though he had written three proposals this year for big-ticket business, he had failed to convert them into actual business, always being pipped at the post by the competition.

However, Tim was a dogged individual, and knew that one of the golden rules of effective selling was 'persistence pays'. He had landed another juicy lead and was sorting out the final details with the 'prospect' over the telephone.

We pick up the conversation towards the end.

'So, Felicity, that seems to be that. I have a very clear view of what you want in the proposal. My next task is to write it and send it to you. When do you want it by?' asked Tim.

'Well, as soon as possible, ideally', replied Felicity. 'Could you finish it by Friday and fax me a copy?'

'No problem, no problem at all. Take is as read. Tell you what, I'll send some extra copies in the post as well.'

'Thanks very much. I look forward to reading it.'

After the usual concluding pleasantries, Tim put the phone down with a satisfied smile on his face. 'I think I have got that one in the bag! Who says you're not a brilliant salesman, boyo. ... Damn! I've forgotten that I've got a Board meeting tomorrow morning, and the visit to our new centre in the afternoon—so I am going to be a bit tight for time.... Oh! No! Double damn. I've got to draft the Elliot proposal for David (the MD) by Friday, and I simply can't miss that deadline. Typical David of course. He is subject to sales targets like the rest of us—but he gets me to do all the donkey work.'

Tim's satisfied smile had been replaced by a very worried frown.

Friday afternoon
Tim's fingers drummed his desk, as he waited for Felicity to pick up the phone.

'Felicity Bardon speaking.'

'Oh! Hello Felicity. It's Tim Granger here.'

'Hello, Tim, how can I help you?'

'Well, life is full of the unexpected, and, ever since we spoke, I have been rushed off my feet. I've drafted the proposal, but I'd like to browse through it over the weekend, and make sure I have dotted the i's and crossed the t's before I send it on. So, I'll fax and post on Monday, if you don't mind, Felicity?'

'That's OK, Tim', replied Felicity. [If Tim had been effectively listening, which he was not, he would have detected a slight edge of disappointment in her tone.] 'Better right and a day late, than wrong and on time. In any case, a day or two does not affect the timetable.'

'Thanks', said Tim.

When Tim put the phone down after wishing Felicity a pleasant weekend, he wiped imaginary beads of sweat from his brow. 'Nice one, Tim', he said to himself. 'Pulled that one out of the frying pan. Little does she know, I haven't even started the damn thing. Well, there goes another weekend.'

Three weeks later
Tim steeled himself to make the phone call to Felicity. He knew in his heart of hearts that, if he had won the business, he would have heard from her by now.

'Felicity Bardon speaking.'

'Oh! Hello Felicity. It's Tim Granger here.'

'Hello, Tim, how can I help you?' Even Tim could pick up that her tone was distinctly more frosty than previously.

'I thought I'd give you a bell', a reflex heartiness in reaction to the hint of frost, 'to check on progress with the proposal and find out whether you had come to a decision yet.'

'Well, your timing is excellent. It wasn't my decision alone. The board considered all the proposals this morning under advisement from me, and I'm afraid to say that yours was rejected in favour of one of your competitors', came Felicity's reply, which certainly wasn't music to Tim's ears.

'Oh! I am naturally disappointed to hear that. May I ask the reasons why our proposal failed, so that we can ensure that we learn from the experience?' Tim, without consciously knowing it, had switched to 'our' and 'we' in order to distance himself from failure.

'I'm impressed by the question. From my experience', said Felicity, 'few ask such an important question. I'll give it to you straight. I was not impressed by what I felt was a slight lack of professionalism—missing an agreed deadline. The actual proposal, which you faxed on the Monday, contained a number of typos, and, more importantly, your total for the fees did not agree with the total of the sub-entries.

'Finally, I wanted you to make a few changes before I submitted it to the Board, but I couldn't get hold of you. I should have persisted, but I was very busy and it slipped my mind. I must say that your proposal was considered to match the winner's on quality and price, but they got their proposal in on time, without an error and re-submitted it after they made the changes I wanted.'

'I see', said Tim, trying to keep a calm, friendly tone.

When he put down the phone, after the concluding 'pleasantries', Tim sat back and reflected. 'Another one bites the dust. I better put price as the reason for losing out on that damned quality control form, and I'd better think of a way to avoid this in future. I know. I'll do a David—no wonder he's the MD. Why didn't I think of it before? Sally Anne is our best salesperson. I'll "persuade" her to do all the donkey work—in fact she writes great proposals. I'll just be the front man and take all the credit. You are a fool, me boy—but you are learning. I'll make MD ahead of that slime-ball Patrick.'

How focus on needs succeeded

'So, Felicity, that seems to be that. I have a very clear view of exactly what you need in the proposal. My next task is to write it, and send it to you. When do you need it by?' asked John.

'Well,' said Felicity, 'the decision will be taken at the next board meeting. That's three weeks on Monday. Board papers are circulated the Thursday before, and I'll need a copy to digest before then. It's my project, and I'll be speaking at the board meeting and making my recommendation. So could you get it to me, say, a week next Thursday?'

'Certainly! How many copies will you need for the board?' asked John.

'Ten copies would be fine, thank you', came Felicity's reply.

'May I suggest that, to start with, I produce a first draft as it were. When you have had a chance to digest it, I shall telephone you to discuss any changes you consider appropriate. I tell you what, Felicity, I'll get it to you on Tuesday week rather than Thursday week. Then, if I telephone you the following Monday, I can make all the changes we agree, get the final version to you by Wednesday in time for you to circulate them to the board the following day. How would that suit you?'

'Very well indeed', Felicity enthused.

We now turn to the actions supporting 'agree needs'.

Understand business/cultural context

Many CEOs believe that their line managers become too focused on the short term—on meeting the demanding targets invariably set. One result is that different departments/functional areas in the same division can end up competing and reducing value because 'they are singing from different hymn-sheets'. Equally, different divisions or business units in the same company can end up competing for the same client base, reducing overall value or giving business to external suppliers, where there are internal suppliers in another division of the company.

This is one reason why developing a vision, understanding the 'big picture' or the overall strategic context of decision taking is seen as vital in many organizations.

It is equally important for the potential external supplier, i.e. you or me, to understand the business/cultural context for the services we hope to provide. There are, in fact, three levels of knowledge required, when we meet our 'prospect' (potential client):

1. The business and cultural context in which he or she operates—so that the service is tailored to meet business needs.

2. The business issues and concerns of the prospect (assuming he or she is a decision taker. If not, we need to develop this relationship to the point where we can move to the higher level). This enables us to tailor the service to the personal business need.

3. The nature and key drivers of the prospect—so that we can develop empathy.

To do this, we need to plan in advance, and ensure that we 'ask the right question'. If we have access to computer systems like Reuters, we can pull out some of the first-level information in advance, which will impress the prospect considerably.

We consider the problem of understanding the nature and drivers of a complete stranger at an initial meeting in the next action.

Develop empathy

'People buy people not products.' Without developing empathy at the personal level, you cannot make a sale. We looked at the PBA rule in

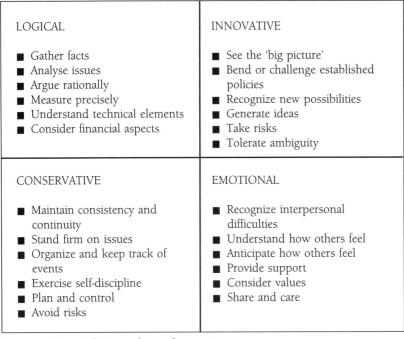

LOGICAL	INNOVATIVE
■ Gather facts ■ Analyse issues ■ Argue rationally ■ Measure precisely ■ Understand technical elements ■ Consider financial aspects	■ See the 'big picture' ■ Bend or challenge established policies ■ Recognize new possibilities ■ Generate ideas ■ Take risks ■ Tolerate ambiguity
CONSERVATIVE	EMOTIONAL
■ Maintain consistency and continuity ■ Stand firm on issues ■ Organize and keep track of events ■ Exercise self-discipline ■ Plan and control ■ Avoid risks	■ Recognize interpersonal difficulties ■ Understand how others feel ■ Anticipate how others feel ■ Provide support ■ Consider values ■ Share and care

Figure 11.2 *What are the preferences?*

Chapter 6. This pointed out that you only persuade someone else, in this case the client, if you understand his or her value system and drivers and phrase the proposition in such a way that he or she perceives a balance of advantage and therefore buys. We demonstrated its effectiveness with the conversation between Gerald and John. John wanted to move up North to set up a mobile phone business, and part of the reason he was successful was because he mirrored in his approach and language the conservative nature of his boss, Gerald.

The question we face, as salespeople is: How do we know what wavelength to get on when we meet the 'prospect' for the first time?

Figure 11.2, 'What are the preferences?', is based on Ned Herrmann's brain dominance model. We all develop what Ned Herrmann terms 'thinking preferences' and what psychologists term 'behavioural orientations'—how we prefer to behave or simply relate to the outside world. Now we have already seen how someone with a *conservative* preference behaves. What the model does is indicate how someone with an *innovative* preference behaves, or a *logical* or *emotional* preference.

Different people will have different strengths and weaknesses; some will have only one particular strength, perhaps in excess—others may have a combination, and a few are flexible around all four.

The point is that most customers you meet will have one strength or a combination of two—the most common combinations are logical and innovative, logical and conservative, and emotional and innovative. It is easy to determine your prospect's orientations, and therefore to develop empathy.

I shall exemplify the usefulness of this model with a case study, taken from recent personal experience.

CASE STUDY

One of our client advisers had passed a lead on to me. He was a Personnel director and had given quite a lot of information—so I assumed he was quite logical. We spoke for about half an hour on the telephone and it was clear that he had a logical/innovative preference.

I agreed to put some very initial thoughts down, and we would meet before and over lunch to take matters further.

When we met, there were very few pleasantries and we got straight down to business. There was no problem discovering the business and cultural context. We spent over an hour on that. He was keen to tell me all the background and all the changes that were taking place and why they were taking place. I was keen to follow through with more logical questions so that all the facts and background could be established. He was keen to talk about all the changes he was initiating. I was keen to come back with some alternative suggestions.

By the time lunch came he was visibly relaxed, and what exactly the training requirement for the key managers was, and how it could be met, was a genuine voyage of discovery, because I had shown I was on his logical/innovative wavelength. But only then could I be proactive and promote my own expertise—and be listened to. At the end, while waiting for his taxi, he felt sufficiently at ease to start talking about himself, his family, their holiday and so on.

Ensure expertise recognized

With a customer, there is a balancing act, similar to that in an effective team—the balance between challenge and support. While it is vital that you develop empathy both at the personal and business levels, it is just as important that you ensure that the customer recognizes your expertise—which is necessary if thinking is going to be developed and added value solutions implemented. This is why you need highly developed questioning and listening skills. At the end of the day, you can only sell what will be perceived as a cultural fit—at both the personal and organizational levels.

You will usually need to change the initial mindset of the customer. So often the customer is pushing for a solution to an effect and not a cause, or is pushing the wrong solution to the actual problem. If you fail, you either have to walk away from the customer or deliver what the customer wants although you know it doesn't meet the actual needs. You may take the money, but the chances of repeat business will be low and the chances of extending the network and bringing your colleagues into play, who can provide different services (cross-selling as it is called), will be non-existent.

The most value to both seller and buyer—what guarantees a long-term partnership—is if your organization develops a relationship in depth and breadth.

I have seen this problem many times with other salespeople, and have experienced it myself. I remember, years ago, meeting a 'specifier' who wanted me to deliver on-site training in leadership for middle managers, lasting one working day. When trying to explore the business driver for this training, I was told that the executive felt these managers needed it. When I pointed out that on-site was inappropriate—the wrong environment and bound to be full of interruptions—I was told that that was the executive decision. When I pointed out that to improve leadership skills would require experiential learning, which would need to last a minimum of three days, I was told that they could only afford to be away from work for one day.

So I turned the business down—explaining my reasons. I was wet behind the ears and made two mistakes.

1. I failed to develop empathy, so the specifier did not listen to me.

2. I failed, necessarily, to use the empathy developed to gain access to a decision taker. Unless I achieved that, I was wasting my time.

Develop thinking

Success is often a question of timing. Until you have developed empathy and demonstrated your expertise, the client will not be psychologically prepared to start the meat of the conversation—the genuine dialogue or voyage of discovery that leads to identification of real needs and the discovery of solutions to those needs.

If that happens, you have achieved client pull and not product or service push; furthermore, clients will be prepared to pay to realize their own dreams!

Demonstrate value to be added

Jon Moynihan, CEO of PA Consulting Group, when talking to his senior managers, said: 'Never, ever, talk price when making a sale until there has been a clear demonstration of the value you will add.' If you and the client have jointly agreed the needs and the solutions, then significant value will have been demonstrated in the client's eyes—and the price agreed will reflect the value perceived—and will be far, far higher than your own initial expectations. Some salespeople can be so concerned about price that they never obtain the price that the customer is delighted to pay.

Jon Moynihan exemplified this approach with an assignment success-fully sold, where the competition was going to charge $90 000 a day. His group had initially thought of undercutting to $85 000 a day—but after demonstrating the value, they hooked the customer, who happily paid $110 000 a day.

Agree standards

Part and parcel of agreeing needs is to agree the specifics of the service to be provided—jointly to set the expectations in terms of what precisely will be provided by whom, when and where.

Meet needs

When the contract has been signed and delivery begins, the following key actions are required.

Display commitment

If you are going to delight a client, you always have to go that extra mile. You have to start 'being the client'—deliberately putting yourself into the shoes of the client and anticipating and meeting every need. You have to make that phone call to explain a delay straightaway and not leave it. You have to go to see the client, when you really only want to write a letter. You have to stay focused and committed.

Ensure agreed standards met

Providing a service is a project and has to be managed as such. Someone, it may be you or a member of your team, needs to be in the role of project co-ordinator and ensure that every aspect of the service is delivered according to the standards agreed.

Pay attention to detail

'The devil's in the detail.' Many a good relationship has foundered because the supplier does not pay attention to the detail. Clients are demanding and there are always competitors breathing down your neck. The relationship is based on trust, and errors that arise from inattention to detail, rather than as a result of some change that no one could anticipate, will erode and eventually destroy that trust.

When something unforeseen arises, then early communication and dialogue with the client will maintain the trust and the relationship.

Demonstrate cultural fit

There is a danger that, because there are periods when there is little or no contact with the client, we can start embellishing or improving the service in our desire to demonstrate just how good we are. We gained the contract in the first place, because we demonstrated a cultural fit—both organizational and personal. We can lose it if we fail to recognize that any changes should be the result of an ongoing dialogue and, if not mutually discovered, at least explained to the client and agreed by the client before being implemented.

Provide after-sales care

If we have gained a piece of business, we want to gain repeat business or 'extensions' as they are called. We can only achieve this if we provide after-sales care, over and above meeting the agreed needs. Specifically:

Ask for feedback

In our organization, we carry out a client satisfaction survey after there has been some delivery. This is a questionnaire which examines each facet of the relationship, and is carried out by a someone who is completely independent of the sale and the delivery. Customers are delighted to talk in a structured way with someone who is impartial.

However good we are at selling or delivering, we are bound to miss a trick. Additionally, because we have a very good relationship with the client, that relationship can actually interfere with the quality of service—for example, the client may be reluctant to ask us to make minor improvements as this may be taken as a criticism.

There is no substitute for a regular, independent audit of the relationship/service.

Implement improvements

Once we have been alerted to the survey findings, we need to implement the improvements discovered in a proactive and positive way.

Deliver repeat business

If we improve on what is regarded as good service, then we shall obtain repeat business, which is usually available as many clients start on a pilot basis, covering only a small part of the total area where the service is needed.

Obtain referrals

If a client is delighted with what we have done for them, then he or she will be happy to spread the good word—as everyone likes to talk about a success story. We have to remember to ask the client to recommend us!

Identify additional needs

Once you have established your credibility as a service provider, you should seize the opportunity to have a conversation with the client about any additional needs and how you can meet them. The initial thrust of needs analysis is the identification of core needs, and there are invariably additional client needs that can be met by the skill set of your part of the organization.

Add to core services

Once uncovered and agreed, additional needs are delivered—adding to the core service originally and still provided. An example would be a client who had a core or priority need for development of all senior managers in the areas of team-leadership and strategic thinking. Once it was clear that that need was being successfully met, a conversation on additional needs may produce a series of programmes to improve the finance skills of the same set of managers.

Develop a long-term partnership

In this final section, we are assuming that you are part of a big organization, where other divisions have different service offerings. The two types of business that are most profitable, because the costs of sales are low, are repeat business (already covered) and business that is 'cross-sold', i.e. an existing client of one area of the organization buys services/products from another.

To conclude this chapter, the four key actions are detailed below.

Expand network

We often hunt in pairs, or even small teams. This solves a problem that many clients face. They develop a relationship with a salesperson they trust and find that a stranger actually provides the service. They, naturally, don't like that. It is a problem for professional firms. By way of example, in some law firms, some partners jealously guard both their technical expertise and their clients. This is not in the long-term interests of their firm, their clients or themselves, as they don't delegate and overwork.

It is important to have as many people as possible from the supplier organization involved with as many people from the client organization as possible. This does not happen by chance, but by the account manager being proactive. Specifically:

■ Involving key deliverers in the initial selling process.

■ Involving colleagues with the skills to provide additional services in the conversations with clients after quality of core service has been delivered.

■ Using the relationship established at one level in the organization to develop a relationship at a higher level. Once you have reached a higher level, then there is a more strategic or 'holistic' set of needs to be uncovered, where colleagues from other disciplines or business units should be introduced to enable effective cross-selling.

Deepen personal relationships

There can be a danger, as in all partnerships, that once trust has been established and the relationship developed, it is not nurtured but neglected. If that happens, then weeds will grow and you may wake up one morning to find that a competitor has stolen the business.

Even if there is no obvious business benefit, you should meet your client regularly, whether to review or bring forward a new idea or for purely social reasons.

This needs to be planned and diarized.

Develop mutual problem solving

While this occurs at the initial meeting, the longer term goal is to have a team (or teams) from your organization interacting with a team (or teams) from the client organization on a regular basis so that problems and solutions are shared, and the distinction between client and supplier disappears.

The consequence of achieving this goal is the final action point.

Expand breadth and depth of needs met.

What next?

As this is the last chapter, putting a 'logical' hat on, this is the end of the book. If you feel that the value you have obtained from the book exceeds the price you paid, then please 'promote discovery' in your organization's top decision maker that organizational value will be enhanced if a copy is distributed to all members of staff.

If you feel that I could add value to you or your organization, then please telephone me on my direct business line, which is (UK) 0181-313-7473.

Question assumptions—some answers

I have first put an answer based on a specific assumption; then, in brackets, have given some answers that other groups have suggested, based on other assumptions.

1. She cannot count. (A Siamese twin, a toy, a pet, a pregnant mother, a corpse floating by.)

2. Run over by car, as he is blind and sold his guide-dog. (Mugged on the way home as it was a very valuable dog; killed by his wife as it was, for this group, her dog; fallen down a crevasse, as he was an Eskimo and sold his husky.)

3. Climbed a block of ice, which melted.

4. Playing monopoly—toy car and hotel.

5. Triangular pyramid or tetrahedron, i.e. three in an equilateral triangle and one on the top of a hill or bottom of a hole. This problem cannot be solved if we assume we have to operate in two dimensions. I learned this problem years ago and was told by the tutor that one of his colleagues was a rather arrogant individual who let a group of managers sweat on this for 15 minutes until one dominant member came up to him and hit him, crying 'How dare you waste my time on a problem to which there is no solution?'

6. No navels. This is an example of the power of visualization to increase creativity.

7. There can be all sorts of stories from the ribald (plucked from celebrating the post mile-high club by sudden decompression) to the ridiculous. The best (again breaking out of two dimensions) is the hot-air balloon with two men in it, losing height and getting closer to the hills. Throwing all the equipment out is not sufficient, throwing out all the clothes doesn't do the trick either—but the ultimate sacrifice does. The man with the short straw jumps out and the balloon, with its sole occupant, ascends to safety.

Recommended reading

Adair, J. (1988) *Effective Leadership* (rev. edn), Pan, London.

Back, K. and Back, K. (1982) *Assertiveness at Work*, McGraw-Hill, Maidenhead.

Blanchard, K. and Johnson, S. (1983) *The One-Minute Manager*, Fontana/Collins, London.

Buzan, T. (1989) *Use Your Head* (rev.edn), BBC, London.

de Bono, E. (1982) *Lateral Thinking for Management*, Penguin, London.

Eales-White, R. (1992) *The Power of Persuasions: Improving Your Performance and Leadership Skills*, Kogan Page, London.

Eales-White, R. (1994) *Creating Growth from Change—How You React, Develop and Grow*, McGraw-Hill, Maidenhead.

Eales-White, R. (1996) *How to be a Better Team-builder*, Kogan Page, London.

Fisher, R. and Ury, W. (1986) *Getting to Yes: Negotiating Agreement without Giving in*, Hutchinson Business, London.

Harvey-Jones, J. (1988) *Making it Happen: Reflections on Leadership*, Fontana/Collins, London.

Henry, J. and Walker, D. (1991) *Managing Innovation*, Sage, London.

Herrmann, N. (1988) *The Creative Brain*, Brain Books, Lace Lure, North Carolina, USA.

Mackay, I. (1984) *A Guide to Listening*, Bacie, London.

Parikh, J. (1991) *Managing Yourself: Management by Detached Involvement*, Blackwell, Oxford.

Pease, A. (1981) *Body Language: How to Read Other's Thoughts by Their Gestures*, Sheldon Press, London.

Scott, B. (1987) *The Skills of Communication*, Gower, Aldershot.

Senge, P. (1990) *The Fifth Discipline: The Art and Practice of the Learning Organization*, Doubleday, USA.

Van Maurik, J.(1996) *The Portable Leader*, McGraw-Hill, Maidenhead.

West, M. and Farr, J. (1990) *Innovation and Creativity at Work: Psychological and Organizational Strategies*, Wiley, New York.

Whitmore, J. (1992) *Coaching for Performance: A Practical Guide to Growing Your Skills*, Brealey, London.

Index